The Refined Player

Sex, Lies and Dates

Stevel Marc

Foreword by
Hugh Anthony

First published by BlackBird Books,
an imprint of Jacana Media (Pty) Ltd in 2015
This edition by Levetscram © and Blaac Jasmine ©

Scripture quotations marked NLT are taken from the
Holy Bible, New Living Translation, 2007, published
by Tyndale House Foundation. Used with permission of
Tyndale House Publishers, Inc., Carol Stream, Illinois
60188, USA. All rights reserved.

All names have been changed to protect the privacy of
the individuals interviewed.

ISBN 978-0-620-67171-2 (Paperback)

Cover photograph: Nick Boulton
(www.nickboulton.com)
Cover design and concept: Steve Whyte
(www.iamstevewhyte.com)
Set in Sabon 11.5/17pt

Also available as an e-book:
978-0-620-67172-9 (iBook)
978-0-620-67173-6 (Kindle)

Official website: www.therefinedplayer.com

Eventually we do not choose what happens to us.

*But in the course of nature, love itself binds
us together.*

*Divine divinity through wisdom tells us we
are not ourselves.*

*The recourse of life is blessed by the hand of
God through waters that cleanse the spiritual
realm in which every human lives.*

*For in our journey we do not ourselves trust,
but He who has led us here, He who has carried
us here, He who bestows upon us His love,
His mercy, His grace and His peace.*

*You behold within you the graces placed in
the centre of your palms at birth. For it is through
these graces we understand who we are.*

– Stevel Marc
Son of Donald, Man of Victory (SODMOV)

For Kwamé McDonald

Contents

Foreword

A hard-hitting, open, provocatively honest and forthright must-have on any reading list. This narrative is bound to provoke conversation – over dinner, drinks, in the hallowed halls of our love nests, church pews, office lunch rooms, over brunch or high tea, at bromance hangouts, and during girls' nights out.

Stevel Marc presents his unique perspective, gained from continents lived, travelled and worked. This is a kaleidoscope of thoughtful reflections – of a man, his partners, friends and even strangers, whose experiences of love, loss and longing are intimate insights for the gentleman who wants to be and do more for his woman.

The Refined Player: Sex, Lies and Dates celebrates the essence of our existence, the nurturers of our souls – women – who have now been given a resounding affirmation as being self-aware, deeply connected, sexually attuned, emotionally wired, and exceptionally caring, however much they are still misunderstood by men. Stevel's insights are as fluid as they are vivid. Soul-stirring.

The Refined Player informs those of us who may not have experienced the perspectives shared in the next few chapters. Stevel's encounters can help us better understand ourselves in the dynamics of ever-changing pressures on our relationships. *The Refined Player,* in purely conversational tones, captures the voices of Stevel's interviewees with an eruditeness. He delivers agile, concise insights on expectations (communicated and uncommunicated) and on a range of relationships, be they from committed, enriching, superficial or unhappy, bringing us to the uncomfortable truths about ourselves. With biting honesty about fears in relationships, Stevel's judgement-free, psychospiritual voice is thoughtful, yet disturbingly truthful, and will make you uncomfortable with mediocrity in relationships and give new perspectives on our search for fulfilment.

– Hugh Anthony

Acknowledgements
and gratitude

I wish to personally thank our Lord and savior, Jesus Christ. My family and friends, the countless men and women I spoke to at airports, on set, in cafés, barbershops and restaurants. Thanks also to those I had random conversations with at barbeques and braais and those who participated in my online surveys – though you wish to remain anonymous, you were selfless, committed, dedicated and kind enough to share your most intimate sides with me in the interest of this book and its "real talk". Thank you for giving me your time and entrusting me with your experiences. Your contributions to my inspiration, knowledge, and other help in creating this book is incalculable – I owe it to you.

To my family: the gift of a family is incomparable. You are the source of my sustenance and strength. Thank you for your love, devotion, moral support, and loyalty.

To my mom, Jasmine 'Mama Dee' Williams, you're my most treasured asset. Thank you for your love in teaching me how to love, how to be a nurturer, how to love and respect women, and the value of self-worth.

To my father, Carlton 'Thethe' McDonald, thank you for having done the best you could.

To my brother, Jermaine 'Jey' McDonald, a di proper way. Wah drop a night drop a day, yute, lol. Thank you for your constant encouragement and get-up reminders. This one's my favourite: "Stevel, you're like a hundred dollar bill. No matter what it goes through, its value remains the same. People may step on it, crush it, pour all sorts of things on it, but its value will never change; it remains a hundred dollar bill." Your friendship and having you as a brother has rewarded me with love, understanding and support; thank you.

To my sister, Sherlene 'Dr Toya' Brown, I can't begin to tell you how proud I am of you and your achievements. You continue to be an inspiration to me and please know that you are loved by all of us. Thank you for everything you have done and your priceless input towards this book.

To Jacana Media: Thank you to everyone who worked

on this book – you're amazing! Special thanks to Sipho Shongwe for agreeing to see me when a friend called on my behalf to submit my manuscript, Asanda Ndlovu for reading my manuscript and passing it on to my publisher and now friend, Thabiso 'Publisher to the stars' Mahlape at Blackbird. Thabiso, from the bottom of my heart, thank you for believing in this book enough to take the risk in publishing it. Congratulations for stepping out in faith with Blackbird and allowing her to fly. I'm honoured that my book is the first of her many children.

To Nqobile 'Spongebob' Luhlongwane, you deserve so much more than just a thank you. Know that you're in my heart now and forever. Thank you for your love, support and encouragement in making sure I remained true to this book even when I feared the worse from opening up. I say a million thank yous and from Kwamé and me, we love you.

To Hugh 'Dad' Simmonds, where do I begin? Like father, like son is probably appropriate; you are the man I call dad. I am the man I am today because of the knowledge and wisdom you've imparted on me. You've never given me even a second to doubt my abilities. Thank you for standing by me despite my faults, my tears and all of my mistakes. To your wife, Sharon 'Mom' Barnes-Simmonds, thank you for your input and putting up with my rather long, late-night phone calls to Dad. Your love and support has been incredible – I love you both.

To Mpho 'Audrey' Ramorola, you've offered me a friendship more valuable than gold itself. For that, I love you. Thank you for being my proofreader and being there through the process of me writing this book. Thank you also for putting up with me when I requested that you read each chapter over and over aloud for my comfort – thank you for sharing in my hopes and dreams for this book, and for just being you.

To Dr Abigail 'Abs' Lukhaimane, your friendship was the medicine that revived me when the walls caved in. The friend who'd rather fall asleep on the phone than not provide a listening ear when I'm continents away and just need someone to listen. For that, I love you. Thank you for your love, patience and kindness in all the things you've said and done for me. I cherish you and everything about you. Thank you for having been there for me in some of my darkest moments.

To Loice 'Tare' Taremeredzwa, you're a constant source of pump-up every time I needed it. Thank you for the tough love you gave me when it was necessary. Thank you for standing by me when my strength failed me. For the incomparable love, care and support you gave in my trying moments, I say thank you for becoming a friend without minding my faults. As you'd always say,

'You're everything platinum, baby'.

To Wonder Chabalala, this book is published today because of your vast help and direction. Thank you for taking the time to read my manuscript and making sure it fell into the right hands. For your help, friendship and sincerity, thank you. Kindly receive my infinite gratitude.

To Steve Whyte, firstly, thank you for designing the most amazing book cover ever – it's exactly what I envisioned. Secondly, as I've said to you on many occasions, saying thank you hardly seems enough for all the time, support, friendship and encouragement you've given me in creating this book. I love and appreciate you, brother.

I'd like to extend my gratitude to the following individuals for giving me their support, patience, input, love and time. Success is the fruit of personal effort plus support and encouragement from people like you: Sonia Barrett, Abigail Jeftha, Jean-Michel Kambaza, Isabelle Kamlongera, Dede Kayembe, Moipone Khojane, Kristi Koons, Kiki Marli, Lesley Mofokeng, Nomthandazo Nyoni, Rachel Stuart, Delisile Thabethe, Monwabisi Thethe, and Nedine Vos.

Preface

We all have eureka moments. Failure to acknowledge these often prevents us from exploring our full potential. My eureka moment was when I realised I was living carelessly in my romantic life, and this helped me change. An unpitying self-analysis made me realise I had intimacy issues.

This intimacy disorder was caused, or so I thought, from the pain of breakups and from all the women who had cheated on me.

I didn't care much for relationships after living through the pain of my first breakup. Perhaps you, like me, experienced the teenage love bug. No one could convince you that you weren't going to marry your high school sweetheart. In my case, I soon realised marrying my high school sweetheart, although a beautiful, romantic notion, was not ideal. I hated the pain I felt that stemmed from this realisation, and it only got worse with the relationships and breakups that followed thereafter.

I soon began to relish the freedom of being single and living life without boundaries. Although I hadn't experienced a great deal of long-term relationships, I always did my utmost to be a 'good dude' doing the 'right things'. I'll be the first to admit I was very unsuccessful at times, and was guilty of cheating on occasion. I was remorseful when it occurred at first but I realised at some point that it had started feeling normal and I felt no guilt. I guess that was how I became a player.

I thought the women I was with would never cheat, especially on me, since I held them in such high esteem. But as I became older, I quickly realised I was naïve. When I learned of their infidelities, I was offended and hurt. I confidently and arrogantly didn't think I'd be cheated on, particularly when I was continuously being told how amazing I was. You could say this was the apex of my naïvety.

I know what you're thinking: 'But why are you playing the victim when you were also cheating, dude?' Right? Well, you're right; I hardly considered the fact that I too had been cheating. I was doing all the things a good boyfriend is expected to do. Even supposing I was cheating, they didn't know this as a matter of fact. So, instead of acknowledging what I was doing, I focused only on their wrongs and thought, 'Screw this!', and gave up on love.

The hurt resulting from their unfaithfulness and betrayal led me into a state of intimacy detachment in a quest to protect myself. I wasn't bitter. I just made a conscious decision not to be in a relationship. Perhaps I didn't love these women as much as I thought I did. If I did, why did I cheat on them? Did they cheat because I was emotionally unavailable and they wanted more than I was offering? I'm not sure. I got some answers to these questions sometime later when a wise man, let's call him *Earl*, told me, 'Cheating has nothing to do with *loving* someone, young man. You can love someone and still cheat on them. A person needs *agape* love in order not to cheat'. He imparted this wisdom with a smile on his face as if he knew it would all make sense to me soon enough. It sure did.

Much later, as a result of a conversation with a friend who was concerned about my lifestyle, I eventually decided to let my guard down again to explore a new relationship. You know when that girl comes along and makes you reconsider your relationship status? Yup! It was perfect and everything was going accordingly. I knew I was in love with her. But just when I thought I'd found the one who would be eternally faithful, she, too, unexpectedly cheated.

In my relatively short lifetime, I've felt both physical and emotional pain. But nothing hurt quite like this. Not even the past cheats. This one knocked the breath out of me. This one brought me to my knees, but not in prayer. This one literally made me live the words I'd often heard other people utter over the years: 'I can't eat, I can't sleep, I can't breathe.' I was plainly ripped to shreds.

It was here that I made my U-turn, my 180°. In the middle of my turmoil came my cure. I finally learned what it felt like to truly and unconditionally love someone and have them cheat on you. Yet, I got beauty for my ashes; her unfaithfulness rehabilitated me. I no longer wanted to be responsible for causing this kind of pain in someone else's life. I had to make a decision.

As the Bible says, 'Get wisdom; develop good judgment' (Proverbs 4:5 *NLT*).

Some changes are necessary for your growth and refinement. If you get burned by the stove you don't stop cooking – your end goal is a cooked meal. I realised I could either continue in fear, living with the façade of loving 'player-hood' and ignoring the pain I felt, or evolve and be the man I knew I was deep within: a good man. It was time to become the refined player.

A refined player means you're no longer a player. You're always the perfect gentleman or lady – the dream man or woman who screams marriage material, even though you may not be ready to get married.

There is an assortment of adjectives that can describe a so-called 'good man'. I was interested in being a good *man* rather than a good catch, a designation based on my aesthetic appearance and material possessions. I wanted to be more than my physical appearance, attractiveness, style or Lexus, which are what in today's society, for some, define a 'good man'. These are good characteristics to have, but they don't make a good man. The making of a good man is within his internal character and not what you see externally at first glance. The *ex*ternal possessions make you look at the man, while the *in*ternal characteristics make you look *into* the man.

If you take a close and unhurried look, you'll see that the independent woman often, if not always, initially measures a man by the level of haves she's accomplished for herself. The woman seeking completion will base her standards on what she doesn't have yet, while the potential gold digger will base her standards on what she desires to have given to her.

In my eureka moment, I realised it was time to be true to my identity: to be the good man my mother raised me to be. The God-fearing man my aunt and grandmother laid the foundations for and built me on. It was time for me to be more than my assets, to take on my responsibilities and be a good man.

The beginning

I was born in Portland, Jamaica. I lived with my aunt, Claudette, for long periods of my early childhood as my mother worked in the capital, Kingston, to make ends meet and ensure I had everything I needed as best she could. My aunt was a strict disciplinarian who believed in doing the right thing at all times. She was also very involved in church. Monday was for fasting, Tuesday was for prayer meetings, Wednesday was for Bible study, Thursday was for a women's meeting, Friday was for a young people's meeting, Saturday was for cleaning the church and Sunday was for Sunday service.

My mother, Jasmine, moved back to Portland when I was about seven years old and I started living with her full time. I still frequented my aunt's home, as she lived just a stone's throw away. I didn't see much of my dad during this period, though we lived in the same city. He'd come around every now and then but, at least to a seven-year-old, not enough. Quite frankly, when he did visit I saw him as a stranger and I wasn't fond of him. In fact, he scared me. My mother soon picked up on this and it became her weapon of choice whenever I was being *renk* (naughty).

She'd threaten, 'I'm going to send you to live with your father' and I'd fall right back in line.

I soon found out my mother was just as strict as my aunt and even more of a disciplinarian. Where my aunt only threatened to use the belt, my mother actually used it whenever she felt I needed a scouring. Though she wasn't as avid a churchgoer as my aunt, she made sure I was in church every Sunday and whenever my aunt requested I be there.

With the help of my dad, she took over a piece of property on the edge of a riverbank that belonged to my dad but was being used by his friend for his animals to graze. This is where home would be for me until I was 14 years old. Whenever it rained I feared our home would wash away with us in it, especially if it rained at night. Though the river would rise to very dangerous levels during the rainy seasons, miraculously, our home stood in place.

My mother was always business-minded. Any single mother will tell you making sure there's food on the table for her child is her number-one priority. For my mother, the situation was no different. She ran a shop attached to our house that supplied basic food for the neighbourhood. It had an open room big enough for about 50 people that acted as the town's cinema and was packed every weekend. It was here that my love for films was born.

While I've never really lived with my dad, when I was older I'd visit him on weekends and during some holidays. I had very little play time with the other kids whenever I visited my dad, even though the majority of the other children were my relatives living in the same yard. We were about 10 altogether. The property was massive and consisted of three houses. My dad's (a mansion in comparison to my mother's), his parents', and another belonging to one of my uncles. My uncle was super cool and, along with my grandparents, always defended me when my dad didn't want me to play with the other children or if I was in for a whipping. They fought with him tirelessly, saying I wasn't given enough play time. My dad was always about education first. It felt like there was a book in my hand whenever I was awake. He'd always say to me, 'You'll not turn out like me, with no education.'

The yard also boasted a grocery store belonging to my dad that supplied the town with basic food types and was much bigger than my mother's.

My dad being a farmer and storeowner certainly did have its perks. The store provided endless delicacies and the yard carried all kinds of fruit and vegetables. And I had full access to them all. My favourites were the cherries, pineapples, pawpaws and sugarcane. I also enjoyed climbing the grapefruit, orange and mango trees.

It was in my final year at Titchfield High that I was challenged by my friend Bob to enter the Mr Titchfield competition. Although I initially didn't want to enter, he, along with my history teacher, didn't let up until I agreed. I went on to win it. While I was preparing for Mr Titchfield, my history teacher invited a friend of hers who was a modelling scout looking for new faces to attend one of our rehearsals, and that's where I was discovered and my modelling career began.

I could either continue in fear, living with the façade of loving 'player-hood' and ignoring the pain I felt, or evolve and be the man I knew I was deep within: a good man. It was time to become the refined player.

It begins ...

I was about 25 or 26 when I was asked, 'How many women have you slept with?'

I was thrown. Until that moment, I'd never thought about it. The question lingered with me and I found myself counting until I ran out of fingers and toes. I was in shock, to be honest. I grabbed a book and began to write down names as soon as I got home. I was so in awe of the size of the list that I stood there in dismay for a while. As I reminisced about some of the names, I began to smile, and soon those smiles turned into laughter as I delved into memories.

'Stevel,' I said to myself, 'you've slept with more than 180 women ... 180 women?'

With eyes wide open and still very aghast, I exclaimed 'Holy shit!' as I stood there, quite taken aback at myself.

I'd never made it a thing, or felt I had to reach a certain number. Nor did I have a little black book of conquests or a women-I-need-to-fuck list. I'd simply slept with all these women for the pleasure of it, with no ulterior motives. In hindsight, without wanting to sound arrogant, the list probably became as long as it is because I am a fairly successful model, and because of the perceived celebrity status that comes with that. This situation saw me become the hunted, no longer the hunter.

In the minds of some women, I was attractive because of my supposed good looks, my charm, my effervescent personality and my ability to make a woman feel at ease. In the minds of others, it was my body, my attentiveness and considerate mindset as well as my avidity to satisfying a woman sexually, and making sure she doesn't feel as if she's wasted her nakedness.

Being from Jamaica, which I felt I represented in every sexual encounter thanks to *How Stella Got her Groove Back*, my accent, and the x-factor some people thought I possessed, set me apart.

For those curiously wondering how these women line up on a scale from 1–10, they don't. I never see any woman as a piece of meat or treat her in that way. I love, respect and adore women. I don't like the concept of comparing women on a scale; I find it derogatory.

I'm more about how sexy a woman is in *my* eyes. I've found that if you look at every woman individually, you'll find she possesses something alluring and fascinating that is uniquely appealing. That's what makes her desirable. To me, this is more important than how she measures up on a scale from 1–10.

Now, you might be inclined to judge me at this point, or consider me a womaniser, but, before you do so, please read further.

* * *

The male–female relationship has always intrigued me. My experience throughout the years with the women I've been with assured me I offered something they'd never felt before (this wasn't necessarily sex); something they didn't get enough of (nurturing); and sometimes something they longed for: friendship, respect, realness and honesty. Also attention to detail, sexual freedom and exploration without judgement in the relationship or sexual encounters.

I kept hearing the same statement: 'You should write a book and teach men how to treat women, Stevel.'

The more I shunned the idea of writing a book, the more I'd hear the same words during the many conversations I was having with women when they'd discover my viewpoints on the male–female relationship.

While living in Los Angeles and sharing an apartment with two female roommates, they kept singing the same song too. They often felt I was wearing a façade, because to them my attitude seemed so unreal. It was fascinating for them that I was so faithful to my then girlfriend even after a year with her living on another continent. They often said how much they wished other men thought like me. They kept saying how impossible it seemed for a guy to think the way I did or be so considerate and in tune with a woman's needs and viewpoint. I just couldn't understand it. For me, I was just living my truth and being the man I've chosen to be. The man I was raised to be.

Whenever I had extra time on my hands, I found myself making notes on my phone and, before I knew it, the idea of writing a book began to envelop me and I decided to give in. But before I embarked on this journey, I had to be sure. I was curious to see if I was really so different and began to interview men and women with every chance I got in the most random of settings. I took excerpts from what I'd already written to film sets with me and asked my fellow actors, models and make-up artists what they thought. Could they relate? Was my outlook really so different from other men's? Is there anything they thought I should add? Was I including all the characteristics they wished their partners possessed? The feedback was overwhelmingly positive and I was even more encouraged. My interviews were always unplanned and spontaneous across all races and genders operating in different professions. Whether I was at the barbershop, airports, cafés, braais/barbecues, the gym or the florist, I used the opportunity. The interviews were audio recordings and I approached them as if I were writing a thesis. I had to share what I found. The uncomfortable truths that must be told. From her to him, from him to her.

You have to be completely honest about where you are and what you want from the get go.

Real talk

I started modelling at 16. There I was, a young Jamaican with the world to discover. First stop, New York City. Then London, other parts of Europe, South Africa and parts of Asia. South Africa would become my hub for more than 12 years. I loved the country and her people, and I always felt at home.

I considered myself a gentleman from an early age and took on that responsibility keenly. Though I didn't have many role models around me, I watched a lot of movies, paying close attention to the behaviour of the men I admired in gentlemanly roles. I took on the personas of these different characters as they fit my idea of what a good man should be and how he should dress. My gentility became more apparent during my adolescent years. During this period I began to acquire and master the tools I needed to eventually become the refined player. I've never lost my sense that I have a responsibility to be a gentleman. In fact, I made a conscious decision to continue becoming the perfect gentleman. I actively took pride in it. I revelled in being a knight in shining armour in a world where such knights seemed few and far between. Essentially, it's here where the adventure began.

We live in a society where many people's views on relationships have become so cynical, tainted by past experiences, that they have almost given up on finding their happily-ever-after. I see them committing to loveless relationships, or settling for a financially comfortable yet emotionless ever-afters. Initially, you may find ways to fill the void left by a lack of love but eventually the façade wears away. The honeymoon phase comes to an end and emotions that have been suppressed become taxing on the relationship; the flaws that may have been overlooked in the beginning, found endearing even, are now only irritating. With the façade worn away, the supposed 'true love' is revealed as being nothing but a failed attempt to find a fairy tale. What you may wish for at this point is a fairy godmother to sprinkle the magic dust I call Honesty, something that is unfortunately ignored during the initial rendezvous because your mind was clouded by lust.

When you first meet someone who interests you, all you think about is the excitement and the possibilities.

Your heart leaps whenever they call and the huge, goofy smile on your face tells everyone you're smitten. You pick up the phone and become euphoric. Then comes the date. You go on your date, styling yourself into what you think the other is looking for. She does the same. And if you're dazzled, you secretly think, 'When do we have sex?'

Suddenly, if you like each other, maybe you find yourselves becoming fuck buddies, and, before long, you're in a relationship without having got to know each other's little faults. You haven't 'lived' with each other. By this I don't necessarily mean living with each other in the same home, but being around each other enough to see your behaviour and actions when your guards are down, and you're no longer performing.

What's your partner like when she's stressed? Is she clean enough for your standards? Is there a dark side to her, or characteristics you consider a red flag? And you've dropped your act too so she's beginning to see the real you and all of your quirks by this stage and she may not like everything she sees.

What if there's a pregnancy when it was the last thing you wanted? Now, for the rest of your life, you're stuck with this person who may not be good enough, or you become a single parent. Why? Because the basics weren't discussed and understood in the beginning.

A lot of the women I interviewed shared a similar story: 'Men lie a lot about what they want or where they are in their lives just to get laid. They assume saying they want to settle down and get married is what I want to hear. Sometimes that's a turn off and sometimes it's what I want to hear depending on where I am in my life or what I've gone through in my life. Sometimes you didn't get laid because I just wanted to have sex and you're talking about marriage. Men struggle with the idea that, just like them, sometimes I just want to have sex, no strings attached.'

You have to be completely honest about where you are and what you want in that moment. This does mean you need to be ready for the consequences of your truth – it might not be what you both want at that point in your lives or the outcome you seek. It's enlightening to take your time to observe, to be brutally honest with that person, and – more importantly – with yourself to decide if you continue on and ensure an uncomplicated, smooth yet exciting move to the next level.

The refined player takes pride in how he treats the woman he's with, and women in general.

Becoming the refined player

My transition from player to the perfect gentleman and boyfriend was easy. How, you may ask? Well, I became a *refined* player.

In each moment the refined player takes pride in how he treats the woman he's with, and women in general. His goal is to meet his woman's every need. He finds pleasure in carrying out this task as the knight in shining armour. This isn't a façade. This is who he is.

Yes! It's a conscious decision he's made to love, respect and adore all women regardless of status, nationality or religion.

The refined player is sure of his place in society and is confident in who he is. He is mature enough to understand that among the good apples are some bad ones, and doesn't take it personally. At first sight an apple may seem perfect, but after a bite a man may find rotten parts, and, if he indulges further, it'll leave a bitter taste in his mouth.

Through introspection he knows a choice must be made. He can choose to continue eating this bad apple and be miserable or even get sick, or he can simply dispose of it and walk away. He knows the bad-apple woman is a single bad influence who can ruin what is an otherwise good thing. By that, I mean he's mature enough to be honest with this woman and, more importantly, with himself. He must walk away if he feels she's not what he's looking for instead of stringing her along for some frivolous sexual fulfilment. If he doesn't, he'll become a bad-apple man.

A refined player knows when to walk away from situations like these instead of thinking with his penis. When the bad-apple situation arises, he doesn't allow it to change who he is or affect his respect towards women. He doesn't feel it necessary to take revenge on the next woman he meets either. He's realised this is a part of the process and that there are also bad-apple experiences for the refined female player.

The refined player isn't influenced by his ego when he's with his friends. And he doesn't need to feel macho – to seem like a man's man at poker night, sporting events or when he's hanging out with his boys casually. He's always comfortable in his own skin and doesn't look to have his ego stroked. He lives by a code. Mine is to be, rather than to seem. I'm always true to my identity when I'm with my boys. I know that, at the end of the day, it's my woman who makes me happy. She has the milk for my Coco Pops, if you will. She's the one I will be spooning and cuddling up with at the end of the night. I'm constantly mindful that she's the one I need to please when it comes to my relationship, not my boys. Here's some food for thought: some of your boys put up a macho façade around you to try to fit in, maybe because you yourself have been putting up a front and they're trying so hard to be like you. By being true to your identity, it encourages your clique or boys to do the same. Our actions influence those around us. Good or bad. If your boy is faithful to his woman, it'll encourage you to be the same. If he's unfaithful, it will eventually make you consider being unfaithful too when you're not happy at home. Live your truth. Regardless of where you are or who's around.

The refined player aligns himself with friends who respect humanity and adore women. He's well-liked by his boys and peers alike for being a man of his word at all times, for being a doer, and for unwaveringly being a good man. He aspires to better his environment and the people he comes in contact with, and they, from their interaction with him, aim to be better men and women, perhaps even unknowingly. He inspires, motivates and encourages without imposing on anyone.

A woman in a relationship, serious or otherwise, with the refined player has the perfect inducement to surpass any limitations she has in her personal life goals. She'll be motivated to be better in every aspect of her life because of the man you are, without any direct pressure from you. You'll always captivate her and be consistent in your behaviour, which makes it easy for her to get lost in the time shared together.

But it's not only the times spent together that are important. Respecting your lady while you're away from her makes you more respected by those you hang out with. Of course, there will always be those cynical folks who aren't on your level, in terms of where they are in their lives or relationships. Don't let them throw you off. They may say things like, 'You'll get bored of sex with the same person eventually'. Ignore them. These are often people who have been scarred by a past commitment – people who've been hurt, people who haven't taken the time to heal, haven't been honest with themselves or realised they're not mature enough. They can't share in your bliss or hope because of the veil of disappointment they're blinded by.

Respecting your partner in her absence allows those around you to be more respectful of her.

Here's a typical scenario. If you're at the club acting the fool with other women when your lady isn't around, why would those women respect her when you bring her around to the club the following week?

While being loyal to your boys is a good trait, you need to analyse when a friendship is causing a strain on your relationship, and know your woman is your priority. You have to know when to draw the line under a friendship that's doing more harm than good. Your boys should be of the same mindset as you when it comes to family, women and life goals.

If not, you'll forever feel the pressure from your woman that your boys are your priority and not her. She'll start feeling like she's competing with your boys for you, which is just ridiculous. The last thing you want is for your woman to not like your boys or see them as a bad influence on you or your relationship with her. You both need to respect and balance the time taken to be with your boys and her with her girls, while being flexible to give your friends a rain check should you need to be there for each other. Your boys may not accept it to your face but deep down they'll admire you and what you have with your lady – that's, of course, if you've been doing a damn good job. If you ever get to the point where you really feel your boys – or anything for that matter – are a bad influence that's pulling you away from being a better man, the man you should be, let that bad influence go from your life.

If you're still in the non-committal phase of your life, stop trying to be coy about it. Here's a little fact you should know: you're not as clever as you think you are, and she's not as stupid as you may think she is. Stop trying to outwit her when she catches you out on your shenanigans. You'll find your life and your relationship to be much more loving, pure, fight-free and fun when you keep it real and are honest with her. Treat your woman the right way with consistency and she'll always be faithful to you. Don't ever take her for granted. Never stop doing the little things. Never stop putting in that little effort on both sides; this will keep you woven together in the purity of the courting phase.

In a longer-term relationship, consistency is paramount in a woman's mind. Don't get her used to a certain standard of living that you'll just change or stop at a whim. If your lifestyle at any point needs to change, sit down and talk, discuss why there is a review or a halt of certain things and behaviours. This will eliminate comments from her like, 'You're not the man I met' or 'We don't have fun anymore'.

Men, you may be thinking, 'If it's so simple why aren't we all happy?' Well, here's an example. You sat there all day playing video games and she walks through the door and all you say is, 'Hey, babe' without even looking away from the television. You haven't even done the dishes, made the bed, or washed your ass for that matter. She's had a bad day (which you'd have known if you'd communicated with her throughout the day) and then she comes home to that shit and you try to get some ass from her on top of all that? It's not going to happen, papa.

But if you've been communicating with her and realise she's having a bad day, you'll be able to act accordingly. She arrives home to a made bed and dishes done. When she opens the door, pause your game to greet her with love and give her a hug and a kiss. Run her bath for her, play her favourite album and pour her a drink, while you set the table for the meal you've already prepared. Order her favourite movie and give her a foot rub on top of all that, or a full-body massage. Oh, you're definitely getting some ass!

Some guys may be reading this thinking, 'Wait … I have to do all that just to get some ass?' Well, that's where you're wrong. You're not doing this for some ass; you're doing this to take care of each other. When you make a woman happy, you're her big daddy, and big daddy gets whatever he wants because she feels loved, appreciated and cared for.

The honeymoon phase in a relationship should never end. But, let's not kid ourselves, life will happen and, based on how you conduct your relationship, you'll either both go through the challenges together and come out stronger, or you'll go your separate ways.

Men, your goal should be to never make your woman cry unless it's tears of joy.

FOR HER

If you're a woman fooling around in clubs behind your man's back or if you're acting single when you're in a relationship, why would other men respect your man?

Remember not to buy into the negative things people may say. They will tell you all kinds of rubbish about how it's impossible for a man to be faithful, for example. That's simply not true.

It's important to keep the spark alive. Let any changes you make add value. Your man still needs to feel appreciated and adored even if you've been together for a while. You still need to initiate sex, lots of sex ... with new lingerie.

Be willing to try the new nasty things that he has in his head – with your limits respected, of course. You appreciate the flowers and being told constantly how beautiful and yummy you are; he needs a good fuck always, his stomach full, with the occasional listen-to, ego stroke and a dash of emotional support.

Ladies, there are a few things you should know about dating the refined player:

> He's there when you're tackling challenges and when you feel ready to give up. He understands the importance of supporting you and nurturing you back to your best and ensures you're aligned with what you've envisioned for yourself.

He habitually tells you how proud he is of you and enthusiastically applauds your achievements. He supports your goals and dreams because he understands and respects their importance to you. He always finds a way to show you how much he believes in you.

He makes you strive to be a better woman and go beyond what you think you're capable of because he sees your potential, and will never allow you to be satisfied with mediocrity.

He quickly becomes your role model: someone you respect and love unconditionally.

He recognises, and lets you know, that it's not just about him.

He gives you the space you need to be yourself, knowing that your path isn't his, but he is confident of your loyalty to him.

He makes it apparent without prejudice that what you bring to the table makes him the incredible man he is – he is good without you, but he is great with you.

Be clear and honest about what you want or what you are looking for from the onset.

Terms and conditions: The rules of the game

It's important for the people in a relationship to understand the terms of that relationship. Even if you two are just friends with benefits, there's no reason to be an asshole about it.

I understand that in some cases a woman may complicate things and leave you in an uncomfortable situation. For example, let's say you and your friend with benefits are at a braai or a party, and she's being clingy. You keep backing away from her to avoid sending a message to others that suggests you're more than just friends with benefits. She'll read this as you trying to look detached and available for other prospective women, that you're embarrassed of her, or that she's only good enough when you want to have sex.

While this may be incorrect thinking on her part and probably wasn't your intention, you have to understand that a woman often overthinks everything to the absolute. You may have simply not wanted to send the wrong message to her because you want to stick to the original rules of engagement: 'we're just fucking'. Whatever your reason may be, there's never any reason to be a jerk. If her public displays of affection make you uncomfortable, say so.

Here's a fact that men sometimes ignore, though. We also complicate and confuse the initial rules of engagement. When you invite her out for drinks with your boys and you're constantly physically affectionate, she'll interpret this as an invitation to move to the next level; hence, she'll find it okay to display affection publicly at the braai because of the signals you've been sending in other social settings. Make your respective feelings clear; if neither of you respects that, then a decision must be made to redefine the relationship so that everyone's happy.

Men and women often make the mistake of assuming the status of a relationship has changed based on action from the other side without discussing it. Maybe you've been getting her gifts, having her sleep over more often than you did initially, calling her pet names or started showing a little jealousy. This may send a message that you want more, that you're past the 'just fucking' stage. Without clear communication, and with her overthinking brain, she'll draw all sorts of conclusions.

This is caused by the lack of communication and, when necessary, a straightforward reminder that 'we're just fucking' may be necessary. I understand this isn't always easy to say because it can be interpreted as cold. But it must be said, regardless of how uncomfortable it may be for the other person. This will avoid any misunderstanding or incorrect assumptions. This all goes back to the fact that, regardless of your actions, in your head you're still just friends with benefits but she's, rightfully, confused by your inconsistent behaviour.

Lines must be drawn within the context of a friends-with-benefits relationship. You can't be using pet names, doing the breakfast-in-bed thing, cuddling or indulging in regular sleepovers in a relationship that's only about the sex. It sends the wrong message. It's because of the lack of communication and clarity that a woman (and, in some cases, guys), if not in front of you, will certainly start acting single behind your back, and eventually, without an explanation, will tell you something like, 'This isn't working for me'.

If she's a gold digger (while ignoring her own unhappiness and dissatisfaction) she'll notice these traits in you and continue digging while giving you the impression that she's unaware of your behaviour. She's about collecting her pay cheque and, as far as she's concerned, you're a dick anyway; and so you deserve her milking you for every cent she can get.

This may surprise some of you men, but there are a whole lot of women out there who are not interested in a relationship. I've always found it weird how men often think they can't be honest about their intentions with a woman. Sometimes she's just looking for a one-night-stand too, just like you! She, like you, may sometimes just want a good time without the complication of a relationship. She just wants you to dick her right and be on your way. Some men may find this intimidating or go as far as to draw the conclusion that she's a 'slut', when it's the furthest thing from the truth.

Sometimes the tables are turned and the guy develops feelings and will spoil what she considers a good thing by wanting a full-on relationship. This is often because he realises she has the x-factor – she fucks him exactly the way he wants to be fucked, he finds her beautiful, and she fits the mental image he's created of his future girlfriend or wife. I know, I've been here a few times over the years. Guilty as charged.

A man must respect a woman's decision if she doesn't want more. Perhaps it's about where she is in her life right now. Again, it doesn't mean she's a player, slut or any of those derogatory words guys often use. She just knows what she wants. We should never be intimidated by this kind of woman. Men choose this option for themselves all the time because we just want the freedom to have casual sex or to not be in a relationship. I applaud this kind of woman for knowing what she wants and for being aware of herself, where she is in her life and what she desires. I tell you what, you won't find a better woman once she's decided to be in relationship – her loyalty to her man will be second to none.

You must also be attentive to the things that can be considered red flags. These flags are different for each individual. When you spot them, be completely honest with yourself. Walk away at the beginning before you're in too deep, left having to compromise or try to change the person.

Tards said in a conversation, 'I can't stand lies. I don't care how small they are. For me, lying defines a person's character. Big red flag.'

Nthabi said, 'Short temper and inconsistency for me is a big red flag. Also, I look at the way he treats service people: petrol attendants, waiters, or the helper.'

Rick said, 'I feel as guys we often overlook the obvious and personal red flags because we think, "I just want to get laid".'

'True … Like, if she has a cat but you hate cats …'

'Or she's not into sports at all and you love sports,' added *Pierre*, *Rick*'s friend.

'I can't stand chicks who are overly health conscious. I went on a date with this chick and she patted down her pizza with a napkin. Who does that?' *Rick* concluded, laughing.

Fellas, be damn clear and honest about what you want and are looking for from a woman from the onset. This approach will eliminate any assumptions or uncertainties about your intentions. Analyse the person you're talking to. If you just want to have sex, make that clear. She'll either appreciate your honesty or, if you didn't assess her properly, smack you in the face.

You should be embarrassed if you have to lie to get laid. Embrace the truth about who you are and where you are in your life. Regardless of the point he is at in his life, the refined player is transparent about what he's looking for. He is precise and truthful to himself about what he wants. You must learn to channel the right emotions based on the moment you're in. You must be an honest evaluator of your surroundings and the women with whom you speak. Not every woman will appreciate profanity or your style of 'hunting', nor may they appreciate your bluntness. That too is fine. Remain humble and know that, like the lion in the bush, not every hunt is going to be successful, no matter how confident you are in your chase.

Always be yourself! Whether the chase is going successfully or not. If she falls for you when you're putting on a façade, that's who she'll see as 'you' from then on. If every potential hunt is a possible girlfriend, baby-mother or wife, being yourself will save you from wasting your time – it will give you a clear indication if she's the one you're looking for, in terms of your personality.

Let's say you're the type of guy who says the most unexpected things in a comedic way, right? Some women may find this attractive and some may find it annoying. If she's laughing, good. You're onto something and stand a good chance of doing one of three things: getting laid at the venue in the bathroom, taking her home or getting a date. Most women love a good laugh and it'll help her be at ease. The possibility of forming a relationship or a regular shag are also very real.

On the other hand, if she doesn't find you humorous or if she cracks a smile only periodically, she might not be into you. Sometimes she'll see the potential for the moment she's in: a one-night stand. If the one-night stand goes well and you were a true stud, satisfying her thoroughly, she may think of you as a possible long-term shag mate or boyfriend candidate. Because you've spent a little more time together, she begins to find you more lovable and takes on the responsibility of moulding you into the man she wants.

Sometimes this works and there are happily-ever-afters, and sometimes it's a disaster because she's trying to change you from the man you are to the man she wants and has envisioned. Although sometimes she genuinely sees potential in you and is trying to help you grow up and begin your reign as king.

This can cause more conflict than happiness if you're not ready to be her king. Your once supposed lovable qualities are then called into question as they are now seen as an aggravation. You may say, 'But, she knew what she was getting.' Or even ask, 'Is it my fault?' No! Not if you didn't lead her on to believe you were ready to be her king.

But, please permit me to ask this question: is it really so awful of her to see the potential in you and want you to 'grow up'? I don't think so.

Now a decision must be made on her part. She made an investment and has now realised she was a bad judge of character and must cut her losses and move on.

Here's the thing about both men and women when it comes to relationships. We don't change; we compromise. In some cases, we take on behaviours learned from each other.

Let's use smoking as an example. No matter how many times you try to quit, you won't do so until you've made a conscious decision to quit and have stuck to it. To say 'I quit' is easy. You may go three months, six months or even a year, only to succumb to the desire. It's the self-will and the obedience to the responsibilities of quitting that is the real challenge, and ultimately what keeps you a non-smoker. Any person who has quit smoking will tell you the urge continues to come. But you must remain committed to your decision not to smoke if you are to be successful.

We all have the potential to be that incredible man she's looking for. But, like the decision to stop smoking, you must be ready to put in the work. Not until you make a conscious decision and take on your responsibilities to reign as her king will you do the little things to make and keep her happy.

Telling her how ready you are to settle down, be in a relationship and start a family, while in the back of your mind all you want is to bust a nut or make her a shag mate, only makes you a douchebag.

These are not the actions or behaviour of a refined player. Why? Because he's the perfect gentleman! His every word and action is detailed in accordance with his gentility. He understands the consequences of his actions. He understands that not every hunt is necessary or is going to be a success, regardless of how delicious his prey may look. He knows when to walk away.

The refined player is a man, not an animal. As such, he is gracious in defeat and doesn't see the need to be nasty to his prey because of the failure of his hunt. More refined than the lion in the bush, he takes pride in his hunts. Unlike his animal counterpart, he doesn't go wandering through the bush trying to find an injured option to prey on. He looks for the finest specimen, the only option worthy of his pursuit.

Preying on emotionally vulnerable women with no good intentions will only make her continue to see men as assholes and pathological liars.

The refined player doesn't think of himself only. No! He takes on the responsibility of representing all men.

He takes pride in his performance, delivering overwhelming pleasure with precision and skill. He finds pleasure in each woman's pleasure and is humble enough to learn from the woman he's with, knowing that all women are different, and therefore need to be pleasured differently.

Only a man who has taken the time to discover who he is can really grasp the concept of love. Only once we understand what it means to be in love, or to love another human, can we really say the phrase 'I love you' and mean it. It's astounding to me how often women use sex to get 'love' and men use 'love' to get sex.

I appreciate a woman who expresses her sexual intentions in general without the fear of being judged. That's just me; I'm a straight shooter and very upfront and forward about what I want. I find it clears the air and clears up any uncertainties for both parties involved. Some women and men won't appreciate this forwardness, and that's okay – different strokes for different folks. Just don't pretend you want one thing when deep down you desire another. If you want a 'freak', live it. If you want a mousey girl, live it.

As I said before, I've come to understand and know that because a woman is forward doesn't make her a 'slut' or supposedly 'loose'. This is the refined player woman being clear about what she wants and desires. I always find it peculiar that a woman is seen as these things – slutty, loose, a bitch – while men are excused. Surely whatever name and view is held of a woman should be the same for a man who carries himself in the manner that leads to the use of these terms. If she offers herself to you upon initially meeting you and you accept her, you're exactly whatever she is. As the old saying goes, 'it takes two to tango'.

It's like I always say about first dates: just be honest about the feelings in the moment. If you want to kiss, kiss. If you both want to have sex, have sex. Why should you be controlled by what the 'right' thing to do is?

I'm not saying you should go around sleeping with every person you meet or go on a date with. What I'm saying is to be honest with yourself.

And if you're single or have had your heart broken, focus on healing and recovering properly. Focusing on finding someone better than your ex shouldn't be your priority; a better and more refined you will make you more vigilant and help ensure you attract a better 'next'.

Bottom line: be clear so there's no room for assumptions.

FOR HER

So, ladies, he's been hollering at you nonstop.

You eventually ask him about his girl and he says, 'She's there. Don't worry about her.'

And you're, like, 'Why are you hollering at me, then?'

He replies, 'I love your company and I thought we could hang out.'

At this point you should be asking, 'Why? Why should we be hanging out when it's quite obvious that you want more than just friendship?'

Trust your instinct; that's a certain red flag. Are you blind? No! Are you so naive to not see through the bullshit? When you choose to ignore your gut feeling the side effects of your decision in the end are never pleasant. The obvious truth that you ignored here is: 'I have a girlfriend and I fuck around on the side. I want to fuck you. And here's the outcome: if and when I fuck you and you get clingy or things become complicated, I'm off to the next one.'

Learn to watch out for red flags.

I love it when a woman tells me she wants to fuck me. Not only is this sexy to the man that's on your level, it also indicates how confident you are with yourself and who you're with. There are other men who'll tell you the same thing; some won't.

A real man desires a woman with substance – your independence is sexy. Know yourself and your worth; there has to be more to you than twerking and having a nice ass and body. Take pride in making your own money. You may feel like a boss on fleek popping bottles with his money, but the truth is: it still ain't your money.

And all men desire a woman to be a lady when necessary.

*Make her feel appreciated and
that you value her holistically
for giving herself to you.*

She deserves to feel special

In my experience, buying your woman gifts for the right reasons is always a good thing and has always been welcome, especially when the gifts are unexpected. But when you shower your partner with gifts and money to mask your absence and emotional detachment, the gifts become meaningless; she needs your physical and emotional presence too. A woman can acquire material things on her own. She needs you to be present. Any material things you give her are just a bonus.

Be with her without pretense; she wants you to listen to her attentively and purely without feeling the need to be defensive. Be a gentleman by displaying sensitivity when she's most vulnerable. When you have a disagreement and feel the need to argue your side of things, do so calmly and respectfully, especially when you're in public.

Never make your woman feel single or she'll act accordingly. That doesn't mean you should keep her caged – you're her soul mate; not her cell mate. I'm talking about your actions and behaviour that give the impression you're not her man.

If I don't trust you and you don't trust me, how can we be in a relationship or even be healthy shag mates? No woman wants to hear her man flirting with another woman, in the same way that a man doesn't want to hear his woman flirting with another man, or acting shady – period. No woman wants to deal with verbal abuse or stupid bouts of jealousy. Nor does a man. A woman loves a man who's proud of her and trusts her if she's shown her loyalty. Never push a loyal person to the point where they no longer care.

Every woman wants to feel special. No woman wants to feel like a piece of meat, just another girl, unimportant, or another notch in your belt when she's with you. If that does happen to be the case and she's aware of it, she shouldn't have to put up with that bullshit.

Honour and respect the time you're with her; appreciate the laughter shared. Honour yourself and the moment you're in with her. Make her feel appreciated and that you value her holistically for giving herself to you.

I've always had a lot of women around me, as far back as my childhood. Perhaps it's this fact that's given me the profound level of love, respect and adoration for women I have. Perhaps it's the result of single parenting that saw me living with my mother and only visiting my father on some holidays and weekends ... I'm not sure. And how could I not adore women, when my greatest pleasures have always come from women?

I've always believed, and my conviction has only been strengthened over the years, that a woman should always feel like she's the only woman that exists in the world when she's with you – even if it's a prostitute, a one-nighter from the club or friend with benefits.

Here's what I've learned along the way (and it took a while to get it, but I did): sneaking out to take phone calls or acting awkward when the phone rings are a huge turn off and make you look untrustworthy. A woman wants to feel like your priority when she's with you. Of course, if you're taking or making a business call, an emergency call, or, perhaps because of the nature of your job, you need to step away to take or make a phone call, that's understandable. Even then, if these calls start happening every 20 minutes, you should probably explain yourself and take a decision to reschedule the date you're on. If you're honest about your intentions from the get-go, you won't have to be weird around her. But it's an absolute turnoff for her and a constant reminder of where she stands, or how little you value her and her time – if you're constantly on the phone, texting or gaming when she's come over to see you.

If you're on a date, put your phone away, make sure it's on silent or leave it in the car ... whatever works for you. She deserves your undivided attention.

Now, fellas, not only will this make her feel that you respect her and that she's your priority, it'll also make her more comfortable, willing and eager to give more of herself to you in that moment and whenever you call.

These statements are from an email sent to me while I was doing the research for this book by an understandably frustrated *Patricia*.

> *He's not romantic at all, and for me, it's the little things that count.*

This is not something you want her to be thinking or telling her girls or mentioning to *John*, who's waiting in the background, telling her he wants to fix that problem for her.

> *When I'm tired, a back rub would be nice ... him cooking for me for a change or even, breakfast in bed ... anything nice and thoughtful would do.*

Her basic needs are not being met. You're in trouble and should fix this quickly.

> *When I'm feeling emotional, I'd like him to really listen to me and be on my side.*

A lot of men get it wrong here. She doesn't want you tell her how to fix the problem at this point. She simply needs you to *listen* and make her *see* and *feel* that you're on her side. Make it your goal to listen, to understand, and not just to respond. Let her vent. Once she's calmed down, only then can you make suggestions and give possible solutions.

> *I love flowers and I've never ever received them once from him ... and all I got on Valentine's Day was, 'Happy Valentine's Day'. He never even added a 'baby', 'sweetie', 'honey', 'my queen' ... nothing that showed affection. On Mother's Day, all I got was 'Happy Mother's Day'.*

All she's asking is that you put a little more effort into making these occasions more special for her so she can feel more appreciated.

You might be reading this and thinking, 'I don't believe in Valentine's Day'. That's fine too. But your partner may and that's what matters. Your job is to make her feel adored, respected and appreciated by you. The same goes for women about their men, but we must admit as men that women are more attentive in this department.

No woman wants to be reminding you of the dates your special memories were created on. It may not seem like a big deal to you but she wants you to remember what colour underwear she was wearing the first time you had sex, what month and date it was and where it occurred. She wants you to remember the day you met each other. It's beautiful to reflect on these blissful memories and reminisce on the occasion every now and then, as this brings back the euphoric feelings and emotions that will certainly help you both fight for each other as you're reminded of why you're together.

For too long men have tried to make it okay that we forget these memorable occasions because we're holding onto the notion that it's acceptable because we're men.

Why should you be okay with *Natasha* saying, 'Well, you know men always seem to be forgetful when things are not important to them'?

C'mon! Your anniversary is important! Her birthday is important! The day you both said 'I love you' for the first time is important. If it's important to you, you'll go to whatever lengths to remember, as you should for any events *she* considers important. I don't care if you have to mark it on your calendar or set it to repeat annually on your phone. Just show that you care. Your efforts will be appreciated and won't go unnoticed. In fact, those are some of the little things she'll love and appreciate about you. Make it a habit and take pride in making what's important to your woman important to you too.

Here's a tip, fellas, randomly buy her some lingerie whenever you can. I personally love going lingerie shopping for my woman. I see it as getting each other a gift; she wears it for my pleasure and she enjoys feeling sexy in it.

FOR HER

Ladies, men, like women, love to be appreciated for who they are. If they make efforts to keep you happy, they want those efforts to be acknowledged.

In the same way that you want to have your man's undivided attention when he's with you, he wants the same. If you've set aside time for each other, everything else should wait. If he's there to see you and you're busy with your work or constantly on the phone, it sends him a message that it's okay for him to do the same. Don't let your man have too much time on his hands when he's in your presence – this time has been set aside for each other.

There are some people who
genuinely have amazing friendships
soon after the fact.

Can you be friends with your ex?

'**D**o you think it's possible to be friends with your ex?' I'm often asked. My answer has never changed: yes *and* no!

I say this because it depends on how you guys parted. First, you have to ask yourself a series of questions and be brutally honest when you answer:

'Can I still see myself having sex with her?'

'Do I miss her warm embrace?'

'Do I specifically miss the warmth of her ass from nights of spooning?'

'Do I crumble when I see her?'

'Do I still have strong feelings for this woman?'

'Am I still angry with her?'

'Am I feeling guilty or remorseful about what may have caused the breakup?'

'Am I just trying to be friends to make amends for the pain I may have caused?'

'Am I jealous when I see my ex with someone else?'

'Am I still in love with my ex?'

The answers to these questions will determine if you can or should be friends with your ex.

Some may ask, 'Why be friends at all?'

I've always felt we were friends once and share a special bond. If we're able to be mature enough to be friends after the breakup, then why not? Some of the best friendships I know of and have experienced involve people who were once lovers. Maybe you make better friends than you did lovers. I don't see why a friendship should be nullified because you were once sexual partners.

But I'm a firm believer that you can't go from being number one, a potential marriage partner, to just a fuck, even though that may be tempting.

Some folks continue having sex after they've broken up in the hope of winning their ex back. This always ends badly. Soon, someone will start showing jealously or something will happen that will remind you of why you broke up with each other in the first place, and, before you know it, you're back to square one. Sometimes we're just selfish and can't picture anyone else having sex with our ex. Sometimes it's for the ego boost of still fucking our ex while they're with their new partner, which is quite warped when you think about it! It says a lot about you and your morals.

John, in one of my interviews with him, stated, 'I just couldn't get over her, bro. We couldn't get over each other, really. Well … the sex. We just got each other. Both of our partners couldn't get it right. Even though I tried everything, it just didn't feel the same.

'With her the sex was fulfilling, adventurous and non-judgemental. I felt like a pornstar, man. We just knew each other's bodies and my orgasms felt like they were from my toes.'

He laughed and continued, 'Just explosive! You know what I mean? I eventually moved to another city and that's how we stopped. Great sex partners, terrible couple.'

He grinned while biting his bottom lip with a look that said 'I miss that ass'. I couldn't help but giggle at his bliss.

The fear of every current partner towards your ex is that you'll sleep with each other again, even if the relationship isn't rekindled. It's your duty to make your current partner comfortable with any exes you may be in platonic relationships with. It's always important to state if a friend is an ex to eliminate any unwanted surprises. Laying your cards out on the table will ensure everyone is comfortable and respectful towards each other and each other's boundaries.

This initial friendship is often broken because one party was dishonest or hurtful, or caused irreparable damage. Some folks prefer to give each other time to get over each other before becoming friends again.

But there are some people who genuinely have amazing friendships soon after the fact.

Here's the thing: no woman wants to be constantly reminded of your ex-girlfriends, shag mates or sexcapades. Dwelling on your past suggests she's not good or exciting enough for you. Not only is it annoying and irritating for her, but it leaves her feeling inadequate. No one wants to feel like that.

If the tables were turned and she was constantly talking about *John, Patrick, Andrew, S'khumbuzo* or, in some cases, *Sharon*, it would annoy the shit out of you. It would also leave you feeling inadequate, jealous, insecure and unsure if she's the right one for you.

Speaking to your current woman about the beautiful memories you've made together and drooling about a specific session or experience (like that time when you guys were at your favourite restaurant and you both ran to the bathroom for a quickie; what an adrenaline rush it was at the fear of being caught, entwined with excitement and pure eroticism) will create an ever-flowing spring of confidence boosts and flashbacks that will make her panties wet, ask you to come over, or want to hit it right there on the spot if you're already together.

It will also make her anxious to do all the things you love, all the things you've been gushing about. For example, when she gave you that unexpected blow job while you were driving and you were on the phone with your boss struggling to keep your breathing intact as your boss asked, 'Is everything okay?' while you were trying to keep your cool with, 'Mmm. Hmm hmm. Yeah!'

Speaking about your exes in a discussion initiated by your current girlfriend is, of course, to be welcomed. When a man or woman initiates this type of conversation, it's often to find out more about each other's sexual history. This can be used as a perfect platform to lay your cards out: your freaky side, likes and dislikes as well as things you haven't tried that you wish you had. For all you know, she may even mention something you've always wanted to try. If you're lucky and she's willing to take that journey with you, it can add a dimension to your relationship. Fuck yeah ... enjoy!

Now, fellas, when your woman shares some nasty sexual shit that surprises you – stuff you've only heard about or seen in porn – don't judge her for it. And if she's unwilling to do the same stuff with you, don't use it against her by saying things like, 'Why don't you want to try that with me? You've done it before.'

Respect her decision. Period!

If you wish to trump her past sexual experiences, focus on creating a deeper level of intimacy than she's ever experienced before. In acquiring this level of intimacy, you'll surpass any sexual acts she's previously experienced. We must understand that, unlike men, who are hung up on the physical performance, women need deep intimacy combined with our physical prowess.

Where men often get excited is when a partner mentions she's had a threesome in the past. We, think we're entitled to having one with her too. This might be acceptable if she's just someone you're fucking and you guys are cool like that. But you can't emotionally blackmail her into having a threesome because you want to experience it, or loved the ego trip you had from a past threesome.

Firstly, you must remember that once she's passed an

emotional threshold and she's really into you, whether dating or as friends with benefits, it's difficult, almost impossible, for her to watch you having sex with another woman. If you want to have a threesome with a woman who is sexually liberated at that level and is open to the idea, you need to discuss that at the beginning of the relationship, serious or otherwise, before deep emotions and feelings become attached.

Fellas, let's be real and cut the bullshit, okay? Very rarely is a threesome involving two women for the woman's benefit. When you're emotionally involved with a woman, you know you wouldn't want to watch her being ravished by another man.

So, why would you think it's okay for her to watch you having sex with another woman? If emotions are involved, she may hint at how insensitive and selfish she thinks you are by saying, 'Sure, we can have a threesome … if it's with another guy'.

She does this precisely because 99 per cent of the time for guys, this is a big no! In some cases, though, she's quite serious about being with you and another guy in a threesome as she's turned on by that fantasy.

Now, don't get me wrong – I understand there are couples all over the world who use this kind of thing to bring life and excitement back to their relationships. I can't speak in general about marriage; I've never been married – that's their prerogative. I will say this though: threesomes aren't something I will be considering when I get married. At least, that's my view for now. I'm of a firm belief that our union is our union. Beyond that, there are certain responsibilities that come with being in a relationship. Marriage, for me at least, is a relationship where we are exclusively the other person's one and only, until death do us part, forsaking all others.

FOR HER

Remember that no two men are the same. Though the chances of them liking the same thing are slightly more likely. Take time to figure out what drives each man crazy and gets him off.

*Communication is of the utmost
importance in any relationship.*

Pay attention: Reading between the lines

Here's something I've learned from paying attention over the years: if she's had a long day or you've had an argument, and you say to her, 'Baby, I'm going to hang out with the boys'.

If she gives you *the look* and says, 'Okay', you can see right through it.

You have to be sensitive enough to reply, 'You know what, baby? I just changed my mind. I'll be right here on the couch chilling'. Follow that up with a foot rub or massage, or suggest you take a bath together or do something you both enjoy.

I'm not saying men should always succumb to a woman's demands or any possible emotional blackmail, but, rather, we should know when our woman's immediate needs are more important than those of the boys or our own instant gratification.

We must learn to gauge when 'I'm okay' means our partner is truly okay and when she's just using it as a diversion because she's trying to be strong for us or she's just not in the mood to talk about whatever is bugging her at that moment.

When a woman expresses her displeasure in a calm, polite and graceful manner, please take it seriously; she still means it. She shouldn't have to scream for you to take her seriously. The same applies to men: you don't need to raise your voice all the time to show that you're serious about what you're saying either. An attitude of calmness, politeness, respectfulness and empathy is an approach you should both take.

If we care enough about each other's wellbeing, we'll take the time to understand and know when yes means yes and no means no while being cognisant that often they mean exactly what they say without any hidden codes. Understand that if your women is being silent, this doesn't equal consent or contentment. You must take the time to get to know your woman thoroughly.

We must learn when to act rather than ask in any given situation. We need to know when to make an executive decision in our partner's absence, without the fear of stepping on their toes or rocking the boat in relation to who the head of the house is.

My view relating to the idea of the head of the house is simple really: there's a president and a vice president. Man is the head, woman is the neck. The head can turn neither left nor right without informing the neck first. We need to be in full communication at all times, as a team, while knowing and appreciating each other's significance and individuality. We need to learn to effectively interchange these roles when necessary, to reach a desired goal without either of us feeling inadequate or less valued. Each of us needs to trust the other, based on the roles we have as a man and a woman in a relationship, without the fear of our given status being challenged. We need to be so confident in our roles that we don't feel the need to raise our voices or beat our chests to show who the head of the household is.

Just as men demand respect, a woman never wants to feel judged or disrespected, or to be spoken to in a condescending tone. Say please and thank you; these show respect and the simple things matter to her. Help out when needed if you can see she obviously needs your help in any way; anticipate her needs when necessary. While in conversation, don't interrupt her. Let her finish speaking before replying. Responding while she's still speaking implies you're not listening but merely drafting a response or solution.

If you want to offer criticism, do so constructively. Acknowledge her efforts and compliment her when necessary. In fact, learn to give each other compliments, lest someone in the street does it on your behalf. If one party is feeling unappreciated, they will seek appreciation elsewhere. She needs to know she matters to you. Let her know you value her and her opinion; she'll feel good that her man seeks her counsel. This also indicates that you see her as an equal and you're not above her. Acknowledge her presence when she walks into a room. Be proud to show her off and let her feel your excitement every time you see her.

* * *

Intuition is a woman's superpower! When a woman is connected to you emotionally, the moment something is even slightly off, she knows it. Even if she doesn't say anything to you, she feels it. She'll wait to ready her arsenal against you, then she'll share with her bestie that something seems off, and eventually she may make it apparent to you. She can feel your intentions by her intuitiveness. Some women may not always use or trust this superpower they possess, often because we men have convinced them that their intuition is amiss.

Admit it, fellas. A woman's intuition is right 85 per cent of the time.

While we men are not as intuitive, *especially* because we're not as intuitive, we must get to know our woman. Your lady wants you to know her so perfectly that she doesn't have to explain herself all the time; you just 'get' her. A woman isn't only intuitive about your disloyalty. Oh no! She feels all the little things that are coming from a place of love as well.

Women naturally have different needs from men but a few remain the same: respect, love, loyalty, trust and honesty. These are complemented with sexual fulfilment, security, strength and encouragement. And communication is of the utmost importance in any relationship.

FOR HER

Ladies, be so in tune with your man that, based on the way he greets you when he walks in the house after a long day out or a meeting, you know if he needs a drink or some attention.

An attitude of calmness, politeness, respectfulness and empathy is an approach each person in a relationship should take.

If we care enough about each other's wellbeing, we'll take the time to understand how our partner communicates.

We must learn when to act rather than ask in any given situation. We need to know when to make an executive decision in our partner's absence, without the fear of stepping on their toes or rocking the boat in relation to who is the head of the house.

It is important to communicate with your partner and prioritise fulfilling each others needs.

She loves sex as much as you do

Women may not think about sex as much as men do but they sure as hell love sex as much as we do – if not more in some cases. Not only that, a woman may be waiting to be that nasty little pornstar you've been dreaming of and perving over. You know what I'm talking 'bout. The majority of men have a porn stash or at least a few X-rated videos and pictures. While some girlfriends and boyfriends consider porn an enemy, I disagree. I, along with a lot of other men and women, have gained one or two invaluable sexual lessons from X-rated films.

As far as I'm concerned, there's nothing to be ashamed of or worried about if your partner watches porn, unless there's a clear indication that they might be addicted to it, in which case they should seek counselling and, if necessary, therapy.

The way I see it, porn is just one of those things for a guy. It's about sex and we love sex – we think about it all day every day.

We can't always explain why we watch porn. In the same way we can't necessarily explain why we measure our dicks, which all men do at some point in their lives. I guess these are just some of those inexplicable, innate things we do. In the same way, a woman might check out her ass and boobs in the mirror after a shower or bath, or pull on her labia frequently because in her culture she's been told it makes the vagina more pleasurable.

Fellas, come clean about your relationship with porn to your woman. It's really heartbreaking for her to find your stash accidentally when you've never discussed it, or if you've pretended to be a saint whenever the topic arose. Don't be scared to be vocal about your sexual needs and fantasies, regardless of how perverted they may seem in your head. A man often cheats because he feels he can't do certain things that are considered 'dirty' with his 'clean' woman at home, not realising that she's dying to be that same adventurous 'dirty' woman you go searching for in the street. She may sometimes say no to your requests but if you make her comfortable and you pose the idea in an appealing manner, she might open up to the idea of at least trying. Of course, she won't necessarily do everything you may have in mind but she'll most likely go for the ride with you.

Watching porn when you're not in a relationship is acceptable. If you're in a relationship, be upfront and honest about it. Be open and discuss it with your partner. You can then, if everyone's happy to do so, watch it together for added excitement and sometimes imitate some positions or scenes – bonus arousal for you both.

While men are generally more passionate about watching porn, there are some women who absolutely love their porn and often have a larger stash than the average guy.

In my experience, every woman has a slutty little princess inside waiting for you to discover. She really wants to be your pornstar, bad bitch, lawyer, doctor, librarian or whatever other character you may desire. Don't be scared to pull that out of her; she's waiting for your lead. Well, sometimes at least. She's waiting to see your self-awareness and sexual liberation. Often she'll wait for you to lead her, regardless of how sexually liberated she may be, out of fear of being seen as a 'freak' if she's the one who initiates. Some men say they want a freak but can't handle the reality of having one. Some men want to marry the illusion of a freak, so their partner may habitually hold back to make those men think they're the ones who brought out the freak in them – especially if the women want these men to see them as marriage material. Having said that, some men are genuinely capable of handling a real freak.

Fellas, in the same way you need a lady in the streets and a slut in your bedroom, she needs a gentleman in the street and an animal in the bedroom. In the same way you want some casual sex sometimes, she also wants that. A myth that some men have is always assuming a woman is looking for a serious relationship because that's how 'women are', and therefore that is what's expected. Sometimes she's honestly just looking for a good fuck with no strings attached. As I said before, this doesn't make her a slut. This is the refined player woman. She is fully aware of herself and what she wants without feeling she has to live her life to society's standards of what's right or wrong, or be told how to carry herself sexually. She's comfortable having casual sex as long as you're talented enough to fulfil her needs and make the ride worth her while.

Ask most women and they'll tell you that when a woman is happy she'll have sex with you as many times as you desire in a day – time and circumstances permitting of course. The trick to having a woman fuck you as much as you want to be fucked is to keep her happy generally and sexually fulfilled by your performance at all times. No woman wants to feel like she's just 'wasting her nakedness', as a good friend of mine would say. According to her, 'Your performance needs to be on par'. Take pleasure in pleasuring her; don't just rush to your orgasm. Don't get caught up in selfishly prioritising your pleasure and orgasm over hers. The experience is more worthwhile when your priority is to please her and, in return, she you.

Don't rush to your orgasm looking and sounding like a gasping seal, while she's lying there unfulfilled and unsatisfied with only your 'I'm sorry, baby. You know, it's the first round' for her comfort. Not cool! Always find a way to make sure she's climaxed if you happen to come before her.

Some men have premature ejaculation or erectile dysfunction problems, though they may not want to accept it. They find visits to the doctor embarrassing. If you have a problem that needs to be fixed, that should surpass any discomfort in seeing a doctor. It's your responsibility to see a urologist for help and get your confidence back, along with your ability to please your woman impeccably.

And it's definitely not cool to make the woman feel like it's her fault for your inadequacy and deficiency.

While it is said that only 20 per cent of women can reliably reach orgasm through penetration, almost all men can. My experience, along with observation, has taught me that younger women seem more interested in pleasing a man or attending to his sexual needs and desires than their own. I can't help thinking that for some women this remains true throughout their lives. They go through life thinking and saying that sex is overrated, because they've never really experienced its pure benefits from a man who is compatible with them sexually, or who has taken the time to make their needs of paramount importance. This is why some women are simply not able to relate when other women gush on about how amazing an orgasm is – because they've never experienced it. Thankfully, these women sometimes change their mindset after someone has come along and put in the effort for them to do so.

I was astounded when I learned that some women don't think it's important to have an orgasm during that first fuck or one-night stand. Isn't the point of having sex to have orgasms while pleasuring each other? That's, of course, besides its reproductive purpose.

I spoke to my friend *Sharon* in New York, who told me, 'I hate having orgasms with my man ...'

'Really?' I questioned her, in total shock.

'Yes. I don't like the way they make me feel ... Vulnerable and not in control. I prefer to orgasm on my own.'

I was intrigued. I think there may be a deeper psychological issue here. But that's her preference and I'll respect it, I thought to myself.

She continued, 'For me, it's more about the power game and being in control. My enjoyment and pleasure is in just having sex, which I enjoy a great deal and pleasing my man, and having the power to do so is just the ultimate.'

I believe if we're going to copulate, we both need to reach the desired climax from the experience – one way or another. In my opinion, orgasms are the ultimate treat after all the pleasurable build up – the pinnacle.

But fellas, when it comes to sex, understand that she doesn't always want a marathon session and that has nothing to do with you being less attractive or you not doing a great job sexually (although sometimes it is). There are times when all she wants is a good 20 to 30 minutes of amazing sex and to pass the fuck out. She's your woman. You should know her well enough to know when she wants a marathon or a quick fix. There's never an easy way for her to tell you that she wants you to finish up without your ego being bruised, so be cognisant of that fact and also pay attention to her body language. Some couples communicate this in a very straightforward way: 'Daddy, please come for me.' Therefore, his ego remains intact because that's their language. It's not what you say, but rather how you say it.

The notion that women are better at being loyal because they don't need sex as much as men do is absolute bullshit, as far as I'm concerned. The way I see it, infidelity has nothing to do with our gender or sex drive but rather lusting after what we selfishly desire, and a lack of self-control and loyalty to one's partner. We must embrace the responsibilities that come with the decision to be in a relationship. If you wish to enjoy the flexibility to do as you please and have sex with whomever you desire, then don't commit to a relationship. I often find that some people want to enjoy the benefits of a relationship but don't want to take on the responsibilities thereof, and want to live the life of a single person.

Many of the women I've interviewed, chatted to and slept with throughout the years have suggested that there isn't any difference between themselves and men in how much sex they want. They also suggest that women feast on the scintillating journey to Fuck-Me-Now-Land that is heightened by the graphic visuals in their heads. In the same way men fantasise about having sex with other women, women think about fucking other guys.

But a woman will have a conversation with herself about the reasons why she should or shouldn't sleep with a certain guy. She'll worry about being called things like a 'slut'. She has the same feelings as you do.

She finds other men attractive as you do other women. She feels and desires as much as you do. As men we think our levels of erotic desires are far superior to a woman's. That's not the case.

If your delivery is polished and you can sexually entice a woman with your words (I mean the real James Bond swag, with the kind of words that excite her, make her quiver, twitch and increase her heartrate), she'll be long wet before she's even felt your touch.

* * *

Brown University's Health Services website[1] states that, 'on average, it takes women about 10 to 20 minutes to reach orgasm' through foreplay and vaginal penetration; while 'men reach orgasm 7 to 14 minutes overall, but average two to three minutes after beginning intercourse'. This tells me, then, biologically, men will always be ahead of women in reaching an orgasm. We need to train ourselves to control our ejaculations to ensure our women are fulfilled first.

Let's look at this scenario: If you wake up in the middle of the night and you're horny, you're already aroused, which means you're halfway to your orgasm and she isn't even awake yet. If you then wake her up and don't bring her up to your arousal level, you selfishly just

---

1   Available at: http://www.brown.edu/Student_Services/Health_Services/ Health_Education/sexual_health/sexuality/female_orgasm.php

want to be inside her. This is why a lot of men climax before women and, in some annoying cases, just when she's about to orgasm. If you'd taken the time to warm up her engine, she wouldn't be left feeling unfulfilled and like you woke her up for nothing. Kiss her a little bit. Eat that punani up if necessary. Again, bring her up to your level before you stick it in.

In a quickie, foreplay isn't necessary and both partners wont always come. In some cases though, both expect or desire to climax. When it comes to a quickie, communication is key regarding exactly what's expected for that specific session. Communication and the desire to please each other is the key to incredible and amazing sex. Make no mistake, emotions matter and are just as important when it comes to having great sex. Some of the best sex you'll ever experience is when you're really into someone, or straight up in love with them.

Many women say they're too tired to have sex. While some women are genuinely tired, for some, the 'I'm tired' line is an excuse used because sexual intercourse is a painful experience, which may be caused from a sexual dysfunction they're not even aware of. Vaginismus, for example, is one of those many dysfunctions – Google Search defines it as 'a painful spasmodic contraction of the vagina in response to physical contact or pressure, especially in sexual intercourse'. It's said to affect roughly two in every 1 000 women between the ages of 15 and 64. Vaginismus.com states, 'Due to shame and embarrassment, many women do not seek help. Sadly, some resign themselves to a life devoid of a sexual relationships falsely thinking they can never be helped.' It's further 'considered one of the most successfully treatable female sexual disorders. Many studies have shown treatment success rates approaching nearly 100%.'

In this instance or in the instances of other problems, we need to be understanding and sensitive.

In some cases, though, women use the excuse that they're tired because they're bored, hate the sex they're experiencing with their lover and feel it's a waste of time getting excited because the session will be over in a matter of minutes.

It's always pleasing hearing a woman say, 'I'm never too tired to have sex with my man'. It is important to communicate with your partner and prioritise fulfilling each other's needs.

Some men are one pump chumps, eager to come without even a thought towards a woman's orgasm. As men, we must learn to create an environment for our women to be comfortable in, where they can communicate what they like without us feeling emasculated or like we don't know what we're doing in the sack. Who better to teach you what she likes or needs than the woman lying underneath you, sitting on your face, or whose thighs your face is between?

Giving a woman pleasure is your responsibility as much as it is hers. Pleasuring her should be something you take pride in and enjoy doing, as this will make the whole experience much more fulfilling for both of you. The selfish approach of caring only for your needs, wham bam, thank you, ma'am, is shameful. If all you're concerned about is reaching your orgasm, then masturbate on your own. Don't waste the woman's damn time and nakedness.

Many a man is guilty of the 'I know what I'm doing' attitude. We need to be humble enough as men to take the time to learn about each woman's body individually. It's good to be confident, not arrogant. If necessary, take some tips; no two women are the same. Because *Katherine* loves one thing, this doesn't mean that *Karen* will too. This shouldn't frustrate you. Rather you should be excited to explore and learn about each woman's body.

When it comes to anal sex, everyone differs. Ask some women for anal sex and they'll say something like, 'Let me don a strap-on and put it in your ass first'.

Some women love it. Some women hate it. Some women find it painful. Some men say it makes them feel gay. Some people won't do it. Some people are curious to try it. Some people have tried it and hated it. Some loved it and will continue to do it. For some people it's for birthdays and special occasions.

Here's where I say: to each his or her own. Do as much research as you can before you explore. Do what's best for you and your relationship, while respecting each other's boundaries.

* * *

It's also important to look your best at all times. It's our job as men and women to keep ourselves visually and intellectually appealing for our partners. Having said that, when you both met, you were both a certain age and weight. As we grow older, the metabolism slows down. But we can still stay active to keep the weight down and try to remain appealing to each other. Continue to linger in the courting phase of your relationship and do your best to remain healthy and sexy! Work out together if you can. Have sex once a day or three to four days a week; weekends are for marathons. While you're still able to maintain a healthy physical relationship, go ahead and have fun! Bring in elements of adventure into the relationship to eliminate the boredom.

And remember, women love sex as much as men do, if not more.

FOR HER

Ladies, if a guy is watching porn it doesn't necessarily mean that he's beating off. Men often consider themselves, or want to be seen by their women as, pornstars in the bedroom. So, sometimes he's just watching for new ideas to add variety to the routine, or he's watching for ways to improve his cunnilingus technique.

When it comes to sex, you don't like it when your man only cares about his own pleasure, so don't be selfish either; because you've had your orgasm doesn't mean you must just tune out and leave the dude hanging, with an attitude of 'sort it out yourself'.

Remember that no two men are the same. Though the chances of them liking the same thing are slightly more likely. Take time to figure out what drives each man crazy and gets him off.

Women, it's okay to look for casual sex with no strings attached. That doesn't make you a slut. The refined female player is fully aware of herself, knows what she wants and doesn't feel she has to live according to society's standards of 'right or wrong'.

Ladies, if you're blessed to stay home and look after the children, please don't let your boyfriend or husband come home to find you haven't showered and are still in pyjamas. The goal for both men and women is to look our best at all times; to be appealing for our partners.

*We must take the time to clean
ourselves properly for our respective
partners to feel welcomed and
comfortable. Groom attentively
and thoroughly.*

Hygiene:
Keep it clean

For some people talking about hygiene to their partner is as uncomfortable as talking about their parents having sex. This shouldn't be the case. If you can't speak to that one person you should be able to speak to about everything you have a serious problem, and one that might tempt you to satisfy your cravings elsewhere. Yes, they're uncomfortable topics, but they must be discussed.

When we describe our favourite restaurant we speak about how clean and well-kept it is, how comfortable and welcoming it is, how well it's lit, as well as its overall ambience and décor. We love the menu to be well designed yet simple enough for us to navigate, friendly staff with a manager who is eager to please.

We pay precise attention to the food: its smell, quality and ingredients. We appreciate the work that is evident of its preparation, the presentation thereof, and, of course, its delectable taste, which is what keeps us coming back for more. And to top it off, we all love an impeccably clean bathroom should we have the impulse to visit.

What we never want to see are unclean tables, dirty floors with crumbs or pieces of food that need to be wiped down, terribly designed menus, uninterested waiters, an arrogant manager, cluttered spaces, poor décor, bad odour and a dirty bathroom.

And so it should be with oral sex. Your body, for your partner, should be a perfect restaurant irrespective of whether you are a man or a woman. Your penis should look so clean and smell so good that it has your woman begging to devour you as she would her favourite meal.

A woman will tell you she expects and desires the same of a man.

Your partner will be able to tell if you're not enjoying yourself while giving and getting head. My advice: don't do it unless you're going to do it properly. If you're not sure about what you're doing, ask your partner to help you through the process. Give each other little hints. Take mental notes so they don't have to keep telling you what they enjoy. Fellas, don't be shy to let her know you love her head-game. Be bold enough to tell her straight, 'Come sit on my mouth'.

We must take the time to clean ourselves properly for our respective partners to feel welcomed and comfortable. Groom attentively and thoroughly.

Fellas, in the same way you want her to shave or mow the lawn and smell good for you, she wants you to regularly trim (doesn't have to be bald), clear the forest and prune the garden hedges when necessary. This will leave you smelling good, looking more attractive and more inviting for her to feast on.

Aim to be the just-in-case man for your partner when you spend the night with each other, or if you live together. This means keeping yourself clean at all times just in case your partner wants sexual interaction. Clean your teeth before bed, scrub your ass properly, wash your groin area like you mean it, use some pressure for those crevices and dry properly to remove extra moisture. Keep the garden well-groomed and the shaft well-greased (women hate ashy dicks and find an oiled dick more appealing). If she gets up to use the bathroom through the night and your dick is just there hanging out minding its own business while you're sleeping, it should give her a reason to just want to jump your bones in whichever way she desires and be comfortable doing so without questioning if you're clean.

The subject of oral hygiene can be very uncomfortable to discuss. Many women I spoken to shared a similar story to *Lerato*, who said, 'I often avoid kissing altogether.'

Teresa said, 'I slip him chewing gum.'

Tumelo said, 'I'll kiss him only after he's just eaten or drank something because his breath is camouflaged.'

Clarissa felt strongly about it: 'It's a total deal breaker for me.'

Many men gave the same responses, and I personally agree with the last statement: for me, bad breath is a definite deal breaker. I think there are levels to bad breath: there's morning breath or bad breath from when you haven't brushed your teeth today, then there's 'I haven't eaten in a long time' breath, followed by the monster of them all, halitosis. This is the one that requires you going to the dentist – no amount of toothpaste or brushing is going to help you. So often there's a myth that going to the dentist is going to have you lose all your teeth or cause more harm than good. That's not the case. You should see the oral hygienist at least twice a year and the dentist at least once a year. If I can see the plaque on your teeth, surely you can too?

I can't imagine making love to a woman without kissing her. Kissing is so intimate and integral to the process that often it's what makes you decide to have sex with that person or not, and is sometimes one of the essentials in the decision to date someone.

I feel for the men and women in relationships who just won't talk about this issue.

Realise that nothing will change until you point out that you have a problem. Offer to visit the dentist together. Some people are aware they have bad breath and just don't do anything about it, either out of fear for the dentist or by just not making it a priority. Our visits to the dentist shouldn't be when we're forced to by a toothache, which then leads to a root canal. This is the reason people don't go to the dentist – they've only been there for operations or when they have teeth problems, and therefore associate the dentist with pain. The dentist is your friend and the oral hygienist is your bestie.

FOR HER

As a woman, your entire body should be so clean that I have no limitations as per where I can put my tongue. Always make sure you're clean and well-groomed.

Ladies, don't forget to encourage a man during oral sex. A man loves knowing he's pleasing you. If you love what you feel from his tongue-game, tell him. It'll make him more confident and eager to pleasure you more often.

There is a difference between a woman wanting to feel financially secure with you and a woman who is just with you for your money.

Money, money, money

During my interviews, opinions varied on the topic of helping your partner out financially. It can be tricky. When is it a genuine need and when is it simply gold digging?

It can be a fine line.

I'm a firm believer that a person should make sure his partner is, to a degree, financially reliable when entering into a long-term relationship. This is for those almost inevitable moments that require a financial boost, to know they can be of support and help out if needed. Here's how I see it: *Helping out* is when a partner has lost their job or they face a turbulent time financially for a certain period. This is acceptable. On the other hand, gold digging is when a woman (or a man), usually an attractive one, starts treating you as if you're a tree that money grows on or their personal ATM. They also always have some story or seem to be in some situation that ends up with them needing money. Your money. This is unacceptable. It's disturbing that some people are comfortable living off someone else or having them help out *all the time*.

I was brought up in a culture where it's the man's responsibility to provide for his woman and children as well as his household in general, even if the womans has her own job. There are responsibilities that come with being in a relationship, especially a serious and long-term one. Financial support is from time to time one of them. Personally, I have no issue helping out my woman every now and then, and when I deem it necessary.

But there needs to be a limit and that limit is different for everyone, based on personality and finances. So, my conclusion, then, is that we need, as individuals, to draw that line if it's become evident we're with someone who is draining us financially without compunction.

Again, if my woman is in need of my help financially, I'm going to help out. But this can't become a habit. This changes, of course, if you're in a serious relationship or are married and you've agreed on who's handling what.

If helping out becomes a habit and one is feeling the strain, though, this will quickly cause problems in the relationship. In some cultures, men typically prefer their women to stay at home and be the caregiver of the children and homemaker for the household, while they take on all the financial responsibilities. This is absolutely fine if you can sustain it and the woman is comfortable with it. But I don't feel a woman should be forced into this role.

Sadly, in some cases, the man quickly finds that he's bitten off more than he can chew. As a result, he becomes unpleasant to the woman he loves because of his inability to keep up his end of the bargain. Instead of sitting down with his lady and discussing why things aren't the same or why adjustments must be made, he allows his pride to get the better of him, not realising that, in some cases, she'd love to assist her man and gladly oblige by going back to work for the betterment of their lifestyle, family and relationship. Thankfully, some men are humble enough to take this route.

A man not humble enough to accept he needs help may end up resenting his woman (for *his* incapability, mind you) and start degrading her. He may become physically and emotionally abusive. Now she's left feeling unappreciated: a burden, useless, dejected and unsettled. If she's not strong enough, she may become depressed from a feeling of inadequacy because she doesn't contribute to the relationship, when he's the one who initiated this concept to begin with.

We must learn to communicate about our finances. Finances are a huge factor in a partnership and, in most cases, it's a negative factor. Sit down and speak honestly about your earnings and expenses as well as who will be responsible for what.

If you're providing for your partner to be a stay-at-home mom or wife and she's dependent on you financially, give her enough that she has a little left over to save; it's nice to be able to get you a gift from her own money without having to ask you for it, for example.

But don't forget to have a contingency account. I believe every man and woman needs an individual account for the 'rainy day' – a time of need or emergency. When all else fails, this is the account that may keep the family afloat until things are back to normal and you're both back on your feet.

You don't need to be a millionaire. (Well, for some women you may need to be but if that's the case you shouldn't be with them in first place.) She's only entitled to your millions if she helped build your empire or has proven herself deserving.

Marriage is a different ball game as everyone's view varies and the rules of engagement are subjective. Essentially, stand by the woman who was there for you before the major deal if she hasn't become Cruella de

Vil. There's a difference between a woman wanting to feel financially secure with you and a woman who is just with you for your money. In the first case, she wants to know that, if necessary, you can bring home the bacon, even in cases where she may earn more than you.

She also needs to feel that you can protect her from physical harm when necessary – that when it comes down to it, she's safe with you. We're not animals living in the bush but she nevertheless wants the more sought-after, stronger, elegant, respected and sexier of the lot. I'm talking about the lion, the tiger, the rhinoceros, the panther, the leopard, the buffalo or the elephant. A woman wants a man who is physically and mentally strong; someone who is intelligent enough to know when to walk away and when to fight, physically or otherwise. In the same way that you love and respect your woman, she wants to see the same behaviour when you interact with other people in society, especially strangers. If you're not wearing a façade around her, this will come naturally to you. She wants someone that people love, respect and admire because of how he treats them. Being the man's man with a machismo attitude isn't the only way to display strength. Your lady wants you to know her so perfectly that she doesn't have to explain herself all the time; you just 'get' her.

Whether the woman is someone you're courting or just someone whose panties you're trying to get into, she'll be able to tell from your actions if you're deserving of her 'chicken and noodles', as a friend of mine would say. After enjoying her chicken and noodles, if that's all you're interested in, you may think you've played her. The truth is, you don't always beat her at the game you're playing. Most of the time, she'll have seen right through your nonsense but still decided to have sex with you because she finds you attractive or, in some cases, to see if you can back up all the 'I'll make you feel this and do that' erotic stories you may have told her.

Food for thought: you too got played. If you don't believe me, call a few of the girls you thought you'd played. Ask them and they'll tell you the same thing if they're honest about it. Sorry to pop your bubble, *player*.

FOR HER

Men can be gold diggers too. Keep a look out!

Her strength and achievements should drive you to be a stronger man, so you can say to her, 'I got this', and she's confident you do.

Why should she be punished for her success?

Many of the women I interviewed felt that the more highly developed a woman is mentally, the less possible it is for her to meet a congenial male who'll see her not only as a sex object or a cash cow but also a human being, friend, comrade and strong individual, who can't and ought not to lose a single trait of her character. I fully concur. We need to remember that we met as individuals with our own goals and vision. A relationship should never change that. Your paths are different while you remain one as a couple.

As a man, and, more importantly, *her* man, you should never feel threatened by her success, or by any woman's success for that matter. Encourage and motivate her by showing her your adoration and giving her your support at all times. Let her see that you're not threatened by the fact that she may earn more than you do, by living accordingly and showing her with your actions. If you're intimidated by her, you won't be able to do right by her, and may not have the personality or character she requires. In a nutshell, you're not man enough for her.

The modern woman doesn't want a pushover or someone who's soft. It's your job to wear the pants even if she earns more than you do. You should be encouraged and driven by her success. Her strength and achievements should drive you to be a stronger man, so you can say to her, 'I got this', and she's confident you do. You need to be her number-one fan, cheering her on and letting her know she can achieve her dreams without the threat of losing you.

You may say the modern woman doesn't 'need' a man with all of the technology that's available – not even to conceive anymore. Yet, I disagree. Whose sperm is it? A man's!

We were born to need each other from the beginning of time. Even within the animal kingdom. Nothing can replace the touch of the opposite sex, being cuddled through the night or the joy of mating while in love. We all need and crave pure love with physical and emotional connection regardless of our achieved statuses. Every woman needs love, even the self-sufficient ones. The modern woman may have changed but not her desires. She can hire anyone to do what she needs, except someone to love her. She needs a man who loves her unconditionally (and he needs a woman to love him unconditionally too). What she doesn't need is a man who sees her as just an object for sex and nothing else. We all teach each other how to treat each other with a dash of learned behaviour. For too long women have been let down by men who walk away at a whim and leave them to fend for themselves.

I don't care how good looking you are, as a man, you're a hunter. Therefore, it's your job to approach her and court her. Every woman enjoys being courted. We need to stop feeling like a woman owes us something because they need us because we have a penis. It's your job to impress her. Not necessarily with money. But, rather, to prove you're ready and you're the right man for her from her available pool of men. Why should she trust you to father her children, or seek protection and comfort from you when she's pregnant? You must prove yourself capable.

If you ask her out on a date, insist on picking her up just so you can get the door for her. Get her chair for her. If, for whatever reasons, the logistics don't allow for you to pick her up, follow her to her car at the end of the date and get her car door for her. If she's comfortable with the arrangement and the distance permits, offer to convoy to make sure she's home safely. If not, wait up for a text to know she made it there. If it's a taxi, make sure you're there to flag one down for her, get the door, and offer to pay for it. When the bill comes at the restaurant, pay it. Even if she offers, insist on paying for it by yourself and tell her you can split the next one. It's nice to get the offer nonetheless as it tells you what kind of woman you're dealing with – she doesn't feel entitled. Remember, you asked her out. Show her you can take care of her. Her gesture to help says she is also a team player. Even if you're not well off, it shows her the kind of man you are. If you're in a relationship with her, pick her up from the airport when she travels whenever possible, and be on time. It's the little things that count. I'm old school when it comes to these things.

Why should she apologise for her success and the wealth she's accumulated or her desire to reach a certain level of income? The wealthy career woman often ends up with a wealthier career man because he isn't threatened by her wealth or her position, and so she feels more comfortable with him. Of course, the fact that he can take care of her should he be required to is very appealing. But, more than that, it's the space, freedom and support he gives her to be herself. The modern-day accomplished woman often feels as if she's being punished for her hard work and dedication by a male who has had fewer achievements. Therefore, sometimes, if you're in a lower income bracket, you must prove yourself worthy, strong and capable of doing right by her, and revelling in her success.

Also, based on my experience and the opinion of the men I've spoken to, a lot of successful women are single because they've been independent for so long.

JT, a London national at my barbershop, said, 'My ex is a very successful lawyer – she was about to make partner. I often felt that she brought her fight home in the way she spoke to me. To me, it felt like she was constantly trying to prove that she's as good as me, which she admitted at times when I pointed it out. But it didn't change what I called her "boardroom politics tone". I constantly felt disrespected.'

If a woman has climbed the corporate ladder or excelled in a certain field, she may find it difficult to make the switch and have a man handle some of the responsibilities without feeling the need to point out that she can do it on her own. This attitude makes him feel small, inadequate or irrelevant in the relationship. I'm not saying a woman should apologise for her success, nor am I implying she should be made to feel guilty for it. Hell, no!

Chad said, 'I love my wife dearly. But there are times when I feel her fight for equality in her corporate field rubs off on our relationship. I have to constantly remind her that I'm her husband. I'm not the enemy … and in our relationship I see her as an "equal". She never has to prove herself to me. I am proud of her every achievement.'

Nicole says, 'I've been single for two years now. Not because I don't want to be in a relationship, but because I've found it difficult finding a man who is confident in himself to be comfortable with my success. I've worked hard to achieve the success I have and I don't see why I must apologise for it.'

A very obviously frustrated *Candice* states, 'Why must I dumb down or lower my standards to find the man I desire? In my experience, I've found it difficult to find a man because they're uncomfortable with my success. Not because I throw it in their faces, but because they feel inadequate or emasculated by the fact that I earn more than they do. They often think they can't afford me. I don't want money; I make that on my own. I need unconditional love and affection, not your money.'

Crystal says, 'The men I meet either earn less or more than I do. The problem lies herein: if they earn less than me, it's a problem because in their opinion it's not okay that their woman earns more than they do. If they earn more, often they want to wife me and have me get pregnant, quit my job and become a housewife while they work. What's gives them this right? I don't think so.'

A woman shouldn't have to lower her standards to find the man who's going to stand by her side as her king. I think the total opposite is the case: some men need to up their game, challenging themselves to handle the responsibilities necessary to prove themselves a worthy king, fitting of such a queen. Fellas, it matters not how stable you think you are or the fact that you provide. The independent woman will never settle for mediocre treatment and behaviour. And rightfully so. She is a queen and you're a king. Respect, love and treat each other accordingly.

Okay! So she trusts you and gives it all up. What happens if you've taken her away from what was a very promising career and then you pass away and leave her with all the kids without making prior plans to make sure your family is secure, or you made some bad investments that she knew nothing about, or you decide to leave her for whatever reason? Now she's left to bear the burden without you. I totally understand if, later, as a couple, when you have made all the necessary investments you both make a conscious decision for her not to work anymore. But as previously mentioned, no woman wants to be asking you for money to do something special for you on your birthday or feel she's financially dependent on you. She wants the freedom to spend her own money.

FOR HER

I must point out to the independent and successful women that a man wants to feel like a man in the relationship. If you're earning more than he is, there's no need to constantly remind him of that or make him feel like a failure. There's no need to continuously point out that you're the one handling all the bills while he may be out of a job and trying to find one. I've always found it interesting that some of the most successful women are lonely, single and struggling to find a man they're compatible with.

Single women often say, 'I'm attractive, successful and intelligent, cook well and so on, so why can't I find a man? Why am I single?' Because all those great traits mean nothing without giving your partner exactly what he needs: they stand alone as good traits and nothing more.

Good traits sometimes come with horrible side effects. For example, people who are witty and bright are often opinionated. People who are analytical and calculated can be rather cold. Funny people are often sarcastic without realising it. The moral person can sometimes come across as being arrogant. The guy who's always mentally at work even when he's at home can be seen as a workaholic. The overly charismatic man is often misinterpreted as being self-centred.

If the man you're with isn't comfortable with your success you shouldn't be with him. No man should ever ask a woman to give up her career to be a housewife, regardless of how much money he may have to ensure their future is secure. This should be your choice.

Your one-stop shop should be your ideal man or woman who has and meets everything you need and desire with the highest compatibility so you have no need to shop elsewhere for either your essentials or cravings.

Your one-stop shop

When I say your ideal partner should be your one-stop shop, what I mean is that he or she should be the one person who caters to all your needs. We all have different ideas and specifics of what our one-stop shop would look like. Within our one-stop shop are different shelves that we stock with our ideal man or woman's qualities. For this exercise, let's use three – the top shelf, the middle shelf and the bottom shelf.

On the top shelf should be the qualities you consider paramount; qualities that should never be compromised in your relationship. You should be unbending – understanding and acknowledging that this is your individual stock for your one-stop shop. On the middle shelf are those qualities that are important but are slightly more negotiable. On your bottom shelf are qualities you can compromise on and overlook for the sake of compromising to make the relationship work. This is the one shelf where all your boxes don't have to be ticked in your favour. You must realise and appreciate that your partner also has customised shelves for his or her one-stop shop.

Your goal is to find a partner who meets all of your top-shelf, and most of your middle-shelf, requirements, which will save you both from having disagreements later. You must remember that, as you enter into a relationship, your shop is now being stocked by you and your partner, and all services rendered will be by both of you. As you stock each other's one-stop shop, you become a single entity supplying each other's everyday needs.

An example of a top-shelf requirement is common religious beliefs. For example, if I am Christian and you're Muslim, Jewish or otherwise, there'll be a problem. I have a friend facing this exact issue. *Anna* is Christian and her partner, *Omar*, is Muslim and neither of them will agree to convert. This is a stumbling block on the road to marriage after being together for eight years. She shared her worries with me: 'What religion will our child be? At what institution will our marriage be held? And, after we're married, I want my husband and me to go to the same church.'

I believe that when we're in a committed relationship, we should have a common goal while remaining individuals.

Let's look at the body. You have the right hand (man) and the left hand (woman) both belonging to the body (relationship) – separate entities acting as one for the same desired outcome. A crucial error we often make is to not effectively compare our shelves to see how similar or different they are.

When comparing stock from your individual shops, ensure that your top and middle shelves correspond favourably while using your bottom shelf to negotiate and compromise. If you negotiate using all three shelves, you'll later find yourselves repelling each other. In a nutshell, find compatibility. Your one-stop shop should be your ideal man or woman who has and meets everything you need and desire with the highest compatibility so you have no need to shop elsewhere for either your essentials or cravings.

* * *

It's probably fair to say women have been 'hunted' by and saying 'no' to men since high school, while men have been the 'hunters' since that same time. If, like me, you've taken time to observe the nuances of a male–female relationship, you'd have quickly realised that there's no set method, recipe or time span that is considered a guarantee for a sure thing for sex and a happily-ever-after.

Every woman is deserving of being treated like a queen.

Every man is deserving of being treated like a king. Show her you're the king she seeks. Whether you have sex on day 1, 30, 60, 90, or even a year later, it won't guarantee that your partner will be there the next day. There's no assurance a person will stick around forever, regardless of how long you waited before you had sex.

The truth is that a man doesn't enjoy waiting to have sex for a long time after he meets a woman he likes and to whom he has made his intentions clear. But he'll wait if he has to. He's a hunter, after all. He's used to waiting and has no choice but to be patient sometimes.

In my opinion, only when you're both in a spiritually aligned phase of your lives and are both truly ready for commitment will you stand a chance at your happily-ever-after. Not until you're both prayerful and completely honest with each other, will you find success, through God's divine grace and favour, in your relationship.

FOR HER

Men are hunters. Once they've set their eyes on the prize, they're happy to wait to have sex. That doesn't always mean he just wants to have sex and then leave either. But if he's still playing the field he'll wait 100 days, have sex with you, and leave on day 101. Not only that, he'll see it as beating you at your own game. I know, I've been there. I've played the waiting game while I kept myself busy with other women. Many a men will tell you this same tale.

How he treats you and sees you has more to do with how truthful you were in character, and how brutally honest you were about where you are in your life and what you're looking for from the get-go. This will let him know there's no reason to lie or be deceiving with his intentions. Say it truthfully: 'I just want sex', 'I like you very much', 'I see a future with you'. It's also okay to say, 'For now, let's see how we do slowly', if that's genuinely how you feel. Ladies, trust your gut feeling. Your intuition is often an accurate navigator. So what if you sleep with each other on the first night? You'll know when he's with you the following day at dinner or the movies, it's because he really wants to be there with you. I'm not implying that you should be promiscuous either. I'm saying stop being shy to speak your mind and be honest about what it is you want, provided you're smiling at the end of it all and you don't feel cheated.

Seek to understand your man more, and understand he is not other men. Show him you're the queen he's looking for.

Sometimes walking away from a relationship has nothing to do with weakness, and everything to do with strength and courage.

Know when to stay and when to walk way ...

Fellas, know when to walk away. Treating your woman right and being 'whipped' are completely different things, bud. I learned this the hard way. The threshold in this department is different for every guy but don't be her doormat by letting her walk all over you. It's said that love is blind and sometimes it truly seems that way. Be brave enough to fight for your woman when needed and strong enough to walk away from her when necessary for your wellbeing.

Women, when they're disappointed or hurt by men in the past, often consider men to be dogs and liars. Here are some interesting opinions taken from the interviews I conducted for this book:

'I have an ex who told me he had a heart attack, was in the hospital and therefore missed his flight and wouldn't be able to make it to dinner, only for me to find out later that the entire story was a lie. I found him in a hotel bed with another woman, thanks to a little help from his PA,' relays *Karen*.

'What?' exclaimed everyone at the table in disbelief, while laughing along with her.

'I'm good enough for you to sleep with but not good enough to be your girlfriend?' asks *Sarah*.

'Men are only looking for a good time,' says *Latoya*.

'Men are assholes. You just want to get your dicks wet,' exclaims *Charlene*, with her girlfriends cheering her on and giving high-fives.

'Ouch!' a male in the group replies, then continues, 'Not all men are necessarily liars and I'm sorry he went that far. I think it depends on where that specific man is in his life or what he desires at that moment. As for getting my dick wet, *Latoya*, that's always a welcome occasion.'

We all laughed.

Women think men don't feel or have the capacity to love on the level they do. Perhaps to a degree they're right. The difference is this: a woman is wired to love. She has the ability to form intimate bonds at the core that defines her identity. You need look no further than a mother's relationship with her child.

Crystal, a lady friend I was recently conversing with, said, 'Men don't feel pain or hurt as much as women do after a breakup.'

I replied, 'That's a total misconception. We may not express our feelings and emotions as openly as women do, but we sure do hurt. We may be different in gender, but we remain human.'

CJ, a male friend of mine from Paris, put it this way: 'Going out for drinks with the boys and getting drunk is not because I'm not hurting or that I don't care. It's simply my version of her sitting at home drinking wine, eating ice-cream, watching love movies or listening to sad songs with a box of tissues.'

As men, I think we often try to avoid or block out our pain and grief, making a conscious decision not to let it penetrate our souls. It's also an uncomfortable space for us because we're more physical beings than we are emotional beings. Society, you can say, has wired us this way.

I'll explain.

As a boy, when I cried it was frowned upon by the older men around me. They'd even call me 'Jasmine's big daughter' when I cried from a mishap. My male peers would say, 'Man up and stop being a girl'. So, from a young age, boys are told to be tough and are reminded constantly that 'men don't cry' when we face an emotional situation or momentary pain. On the other hand, when women are in emotional pain, they are tended to. Therefore, as a man, the last thing we want is to be seen as 'unmanly' or a 'baby', and so we're forced to postpone and suppress our emotions and get on with life, in some cases, just to be strong for those around us and because that's what's expected of us.

Some women will say, 'Baby, it's okay to let me see you cry.' Some men give in to this request and find it liberating to just cry it out without the worry of feeling judged by his woman. Others are cautious to start something they can't turn off. There's also the fear of not knowing the rules: cry too often and it starts becoming very unattractive. Some women take advantage of the situation, too. The moment a man lets any measure of tears out, it's used against him later in a fight or disagreement – she tells him he's too soft or isn't manly enough.

Seek to understand your woman more. She's not other women; she's your one-stop shop.

* * *

'When is it time to walk away from your relationship?'

'When is it time to stay?'

These are questions I would often ask myself before I got help from my therapist after a breakup that left me shaken to my core. My therapist, realising I had lost a bit of myself in one of my relationships, said, 'Stevel, sometimes walking away from a relationship has nothing to do with weakness, and everything to do with strength and courage. We walk away not because we want others to realise our worth and value but because we finally see our own value.'

My self-analysis, with the help of my interviews, taught me that I was perhaps a bit naïve at times. Too forgiving. Too understanding. Too selfless. I needed to learn how to strike a balance between knowing when to walk away, when to stay and when to fight for a relationship. It's about self-value. We need to be honest about when we're being taken advantage of because we're too understanding and giving. We need to learn to nip it as it happens and not ignore discomfort caused by our partner's actions. I've found that we often stick around even when it's bad for us because we're hopeful. We have a desire to stay true to the commitment we've made to our partners and ourselves when we say forever at the altar, or in our quest to get to the altar. It is the fear of failing at yet another relationship. Without realising it, we're so far in that we start making excuses for our partners. We say,

'Well, it's still better than my previous relationships. They'll come around.' We start lying on our partner's behalf to our friends and loved ones to protect them from being viewed a certain way.

I remember being so committed and determined in the relationship I mentioned above that it didn't matter what my partner did or said – I'd try to fix it.

When she messed up, I'd say to myself, 'Stevel, you made a commitment to yourself and *Natalie* never to leave her. You can't keep running away from your relationships every time things get rocky.'

And to her, when I messed up, I'd say, '*Natalie*, we said forever; we can fix this … let's work things out.' She'd say the same when she did me wrong.

I'd see what were, for me, blatant red flags and ignore them.

Like when she cheated on me. I knew deep down it would continue because women, unlike men, aren't susceptible to cheating. It's not within their nature to do so. So when they do cheat, they'll continue to do so with the same person or others because they've lost that thing that kept them from doing so to begin with. Though a cheater may stop cheating during the relationship, if what led her to cheat continues, she'll be tempted to cheat again or continue cheating. Here's the thing though: women never just cheat. She'll show you her intentions to cheat through her actions and behaviour because of something you're not doing or because of something you've been doing that she doesn't appreciate. As was the case with *Natalie*. I ignored the warning signs and she cheated several more times. I'd feel it without her telling me but when I'd question her, she'd vehemently deny it. Eventually, she'd confess when asked with the evidence stacked up against her.

My spiritual connection was so deep that I'd feel her infidelity as it occurred. I'd often say to her: '*Natalie*, I don't need to be around you to see what you're doing. I see you through God's eyes.' Thinking I was just making up stories, she'd laugh at me, almost as if to say, 'Yeah, right'. This changed when I once called her immediately after one of her moments of infidelity to play back to her what she'd just done. I'd seen it as if I were watching a film. My belief is that all of humanity is a large book written by one Author and so we're all connected in one way or another. Depending on how close you are to the Author, supernaturally He gives you glimpses through His eyes, just as it had occurred to me in that moment.

Though I was in pain and knew it was time to walk away, I chose to ignore my gut feelings and instead looked back at the years we'd given each other and thought, 'Better the devil I know than starting all over again. I've invested too much of me to just walk away now.' I thought, 'Surely this is the universe's way of catching up with me for all the cheating I've done in my past.' Except it wasn't. In fact, this was the universe telling me it was time to walk away. God doesn't use our past against us and two wrongs don't make a right. Everything has to happen in the time allotted by the Author and He'll keep repeating the same chapter for us until we've learned the lesson or are ready for our next task. As Louise L. Hay says in her book, *You Can Heal Your Life*, 'Some people are not ready, and there is no judgment. We all begin to make our changes in the right time, space, and sequence for us.'

I realised I was in too deep and it was time to walk away when *Natalie* and I kept having the exact arguments over and over again. I couldn't remember the last time I had had a meaningful conversation with her. She had become disrespectful and respect is the basis of any relationship. Without it, there's always tension and resentment. Our laughter had almost disappeared and the phone calls were a matter of nicety. I found myself fantasising about when the sex used to be exciting. I realised I was slowly growing to despise her for her actions and for the person she'd become. But, as the Author would have it in His perfect timing, just then, as I had the strength and had reached my limit, *Natalie* called to set me free.

She said, 'My therapist said something that got me thinking … I think we should break up.'

'What did she say?' I asked, with my heart pounding out of my chest and the Johannesburg Highveld air suddenly seeming extra thin as I struggled to breathe.

'She says I can't keep using you as a crutch. I can't learn if you forgive me for everything every time I mess up. I can't feel the consequences of my actions.'

I replied, 'I've been telling you that for a while now. It's as if you're holding onto me with one hand while you see what else is available and if that doesn't work out, you have me to fall back on.'

'Yes! I know …' she concurred. 'That's why I'd prefer we broke up now before you hate me. Before I turn you into a person you're not. You're a good man and you deserve better. I need to find myself. I'd rather leave you now before I completely ruin any hope of a future with you should our paths cross again.'

Even though I knew all she had said was true, I was left feeling devastated and helpless as I saw everything crumble before me. I called her back that evening. I said calmly, 'You've fought for me several times in the past when I've broken up with you … This is me fighting for you now. I know what your therapist said, but is this what you want?' I was hoping she'd have changed her mind by then.

'It's not what I want, but I think it's what's best for us,' she said.

'Okay,' I concluded.

The first call that followed was to my best friend and the person most realistic about life that I know: my mother. I called her for strength and she gave me just that without prejudice. She reminded me what she's always taught me from an early age: self-worth.

'Son,' she started, then paused to take a breath and then exhale. I could hear that she felt my pain as all mothers do when their children are hurt. 'I'm sorry for your pain. But remember your worth and be strong. As I've always told you over the years: never fight for a woman who doesn't want to be fought for. You're a king ... and only a queen can handle the values present within a king. When a woman tells you she doesn't want you anymore, don't question it, and don't try to convince her otherwise. That's not the time to remind her of your value, of the good man you are or what you've done for her. Be still, based on the foundation you've laid for her in the relationship and how you nurtured her. In due time, she'll remember all those things and come back to you if you did a good job. Focus on whether or not you want her back by your side when she comes knocking. I raised a king in you. Never forget that!' As usual, every word was precise and measured.

I told her how much I love her, thanked her for her prayers and her royal wisdom, and said goodnight to her in Jamaica from South Africa.

* * *

I met up with *Priya*, who is from India, while we were visiting a mutual friend in New York. She shared similar views to my mom, saying, 'A man must know his value. If you beg me to stay with you, then I know you can't do without me and I may take advantage of that in one form or another. Often women think the grass is greener on the other side because of a rut in the relationship or because there's a new guy we're flirting with who offers excitement or whatever our present relationship isn't offering. But we soon realise, like in my case, the grass wasn't greener on the other side after all. I went back to my guy begging and after six months he took me back. Though we've been married now for eight years, it's a lesson I've never forgotten. I could have lost the love of my life because of the 20 per cent that I thought was missing when he was 80 per cent perfection. It's also important to note that I now get that 20 per cent from him. It only took me speaking up in the relationship about what I wanted. Communicate with your partner; you may find that you already have exactly what you're looking for.'

On another occasion, *Blake,* visiting Los Angeles from Texas, told me, 'As obvious as it is, not a lot of us guys "get it", especially when we're "in love". My rule is to never let a woman tell me more than once that she doesn't want me because of her own issues. I know I'm a good man and I always treat my women right. Once a woman tells you she's through, believe it and move on. A lot of folks, men and women, tend to think we can change people's minds or hearts, but the reality is that when someone tells you it's done, it's done.'

Is it that we're too hopeful when deep down we know a relationship is doomed? Could it be that we take commitment too seriously when it's one-sided and aren't honest about that fact with ourselves? Why do we ignore being taken for granted when it's often so obvious? Could it be that we're afraid of change or of having had another failed relationship? Is it that our vision is just too clouded with emotion? Isn't it interesting how, often, everyone around us sees the truth of the situation and tells us that it's time to walk away, yet we still hold on? Friends and relatives go out of their way to show us that it's time to move on, sometimes at the risk of a fight or losing our friendship, because they care. Somehow we remain stubborn about letting go.

In one of my interviews, *Louise* gave me some insight: 'I think all of us ignore the signs of "craziness" at the beginning of any affiliation. Most of the time after a relationship has ended, I go through a post-mortem phase. I sit down and recall every conversation, remark or situation from the relationship, and every time I always have to ask myself, "What the fuck where you thinking?", because for some reason everything becomes clear when you're no longer clouded with emotions or infatuation.'

I've uncovered a number of reasons people might have wanted to walk away:

When your relationship feels stuck:

Jaqueline told me, 'Your relationship is stuck when you no longer feel or see a future with your partner. This is when you both argue about the same things over and over again. You no longer have respect or consideration for one another, and most of your time is spent arguing about the same mess, which is usually nothing. The laughter goes and the tension is thick enough to cut with a knife. You go into survival mode and you start fights so you can get by and silence becomes the game. You pray to God you're not in a car driving long distance when a fight happens.'

When it starts getting physical:

Here's *Corey*'s experience: 'Usually it starts with the arguments and then, eventually, one of you feels the need to restrain the other – whether by the holding of an arm, the pulling of hair or shaking your partner violently. Sometimes you just downright slap them or get slapped. This is a sign it's time for you to leave. Physical violence should never be tolerated. There's no better sign that it's time to walk away.'

When you start stepping out on each other:

Isabelle said, 'My belief is that a relationship is between two people and not more than that, unless stated otherwise at the beginning of the relationship. If you stick around after knowing that your partner cheated on you, you set a standard: they'll keep cheating. If you're going to cheat on me, I don't want to know. As a woman, if I cheat on you, it's been long coming because of my unhappiness. I'm most likely over the relationship and I'll keep cheating on you.'

When you stop trusting your partner:

Lebo shared her experiences: 'There's nothing worse than dealing with a person who thinks they always have to extend the truth a little bit, for this shows that they don't trust you or respect you enough. This just creates a lot of trust issues, so it's better to call it quits. Once I doubt something you've done, then it's time to end it.

Playing detective in a relationship is not my cup of tea. It's exhausting and annoying. A relationship should be about two consenting adults. Once one starts feeling like they're being forced to be there, or that they're forcing their partner to be there, it's time to go.

When you're being taken for granted or when love hurts:

Priscilla said, 'A relationship should be about loving, caring, giving and receiving. However, when it starts being one-sided and all you do is out of demand instead of being appreciated, then it's time to leave. I've never understood the concept that love hurts – love must be, above all, the most beautiful feeling in the world but is often confused with pain. I think when you spend too much time crying about a relationship or "your person" then clearly this is no longer love. My belief is that when you love someone you shield them from all the hurt and want to see them smile. But when you become the reason for their misery then it's time to let go.'

If there's emotional blackmail:

Joanna told me, 'When one partner preys on the other's emotions for their own gain it's time to bounce. If emotional blackmail or emotional abuse is used, I see that as a flaw within my partner's character and it's not healthy for me. Because I love you and you know my weaknesses it doesn't mean you should use that against me. Time to leave.'

The issue becomes even more difficult in the event of marriage. *Sandra* said, 'Knowing that you should end things and actually ending them is a process, a journey, which takes immense courage and strength. One may hold back because of one's religious beliefs. In the Christian faith there are some who follow the Old Testament. Therefore there are cases of people who are victims of verbal, emotional or physical abuse, yet they stay married because the Bible says they must.'

Luke told me, 'I've been told I'm a coward for not having the guts to leave my wife. I know I'm not happy. I don't want to be looked down on by my family. I keep hoping that she'll change. Perhaps I'm living under the delusion that she'll eventually change her behaviour.'

It seems to me that people stay in bad relationships mainly out of the fear of change. Calling it quits means that things would have to be different and change is not a very comfortable thing. The fear of failure also comes into it; a prolonged relationship can be seen as an achievement for some. Acknowledging that things are not working and seeking a different path may be seen by some as a failure.

Monique, a friend and relationship therapist from South Africa, explained, 'Stevel, loneliness is a big one. Many couples stay together because they feel like they have to have a partner, not because they're in love with each other – keeping up appearances; not wanting to seem like a "have not". Look how many women are married for reasons apart from love and who find themselves in loveless and empty marriages. Some claim to stay for the children. This morning, one of my clients shared that, though she wants to leave the abusive relationship she's in, she thinks it's better to stick with the devil she knows. She explained that getting used to being ill-treated makes you become crippled by the fear that others might treat you even worse than what you're used to.' She paused to take a sip of her coffee. 'There are several reasons why people may hold back from calling it quits. The term "quit" has a negative connotation, one which suggests that the case could have been "won".'

She paused again to take another sip of her coffee and continued, 'Then there's the guilt that follows – as a Christian, guilt from not believing in divorce at all. Guilt based on whether God approves of our decision. I encourage my clients to choose happiness and, where necessary, take steps towards self-forgiveness. Bravery is needed in all phases.'

Debbie, a heart surgeon I met on a flight from London, shared this with me: 'How do we know when it's enough? I think it varies for each person. But for me it was the point where staying meant losing myself completely. I had to fully love myself and then evaluate the relationship and how I, the woman, was fairing. I even tried self-sacrificing love but that cost me energy, mental stability and far too much emotional turmoil. I was suffering and barely alive. I then examined whether the relationship I was staying in reflected love from my partner, and whether it was what I deserved. When we truly love we are guided by the principles in the Bible from Corinthians and so on. By these same standards we should measure the love we receive from our partner. I quit when there was no hope for change.

'It was better to let go than stay and grow bitter,' she added softly, as she delved into her past. 'The love I gave wasn't bad, but perhaps I loved him more by setting him free – to seek that which he seemed to have been after. This also freed me to relearn who I was and who I wanted to be,' she continued, a little teary-eyed yet proudly, with a half-smile.

Jonathan, still obviously saddened by his divorce, shared this with me: 'I realised simply loving wasn't enough. I didn't want to look back and question my decision to stay. I didn't want that. This was my wife. My forevermore. I'd ask myself why I wasn't happy.

'Looking back at it, I still accept that it was the right decision to get married at the time. We were in love and everything was perfect,' he continue after pulling himself together. 'After a few failed ventures that brought pressure on our marriage and infidelity from both sides, I needed to end things because we both deserved better. I was no longer a person who could love her as much as I did in the beginning and it wouldn't have been fair to stick around knowing this.'

The conclusion I arrived at is this: relationships are hard work. Whether you decide to stay or leave your relationship, the choice is entirely yours and either choice is valid. It's your truth. Be honest about what your relationship is and what you want. On-again, off-again relationships often remain that way and won't ever change. You shouldn't let your comfort become your kryptonite – you deserve better. Don't completely tune out friends or loved ones who voice their concern; if you don't value your friends' opinions then it's probably time to get some new ones. Strike a balance between your own honest self-analysis and an outsider's perspective. Dissatisfaction will happen from time to time but it's important to discuss these issues with your partner to resolve them. However, if you feel more frustration than happiness, or that your partner isn't listening to you, then chances are your relationship is in serious trouble. If you've been working on the relationship for a time and there's been no change for the better, it's time to walk away. Don't allow the fear of change and the fear of loneliness keep you in denial or drive you to make excuses for your partner. The key to getting what you want from your relationship and love life is about communicating with your partner. As *Priya* put it, 'You may find you already have exactly what you're looking for.'

Walk-away checklist:

✓ Trust has gone out the window.

✓ We are emotionally disconnected.

✓ We are disrespectful toward each other.

✓ We keep arguing about the same thing over and over.

✓ The laughter has dried up, leaving only tension.

✓ The sex has become dissatisfactory.

✓ Phone calls are uncomfortable.

✓ We're only in the relationship out of the fear of change or to keep up appearances.

✓ Our values and future ambitions aren't the same.

✓ The relationship is abusive: verbally, emotionally, physically or otherwise.

*Often a man's greatness is the
result of the woman in his life.
Her good qualities, behaviour,
strength and actions complement his,
and help to make him great.*

The *ezer neged*:
Your help, your source
of strength

'We must learn the lesson from our misfortunes, otherwise our past mishaps were pointless,' said *Megan*, the perfect stranger.

This particular conversation started several years after we first became Facebook friends. I asked her when she planned to have a child of her own. It was in that very moment that her response confirmed what I've always felt so many women struggle with in today's society – the balance between being the 'good wife' and the feminist.

She responded, 'Stevel, I'm preparing to be a wife first before having any children, though I am presently single. With ruthless introspection, I've realised that I have some feminist tendencies, which, in my opinion, prevent me from being the *ezer* that God created me to be. So, for now, I'm painfully learning what submission truly is without feeling like I'm a child or a slave. I've always been a rebel in my past relationships, or so I've been told.'

She explained further, 'I am reminded of the importance of being a woman. I am a nurturer, I am sensitive, I am delicate and I am strong. As women, we must find the beauty in that, irrespective of our "Boaz".[2] It's our responsibility to define and refine ourselves to be the best *ezer* we can be for our Boaz – we must have our own womanhood identified as the woman we've decided to be and not who society says we should be. Every Ruth and Boaz will be different, but the one thing that should remain is *agape* love[3] and respect for each other. If I truly know who I am, then I am not bothered by who everyone else thinks I should be. I must know who I am as a wife before I can be a mother. If I know who I am, then I won't have to be defined by my husband.'

This really made me think: for us to only look at the word *ezer* or *helper* in a domestic manner is rather careless of us. The term is more complex than it seems.

---

2   Boaz and Ruth are husband and wife in the Book of Ruth – one of the great love stories.

3   *Agape* is one of the several Greek words for *love*. There is also *phileo*, or brotherly love; *eros*: erotic love; and *storge*, which is love between family members.

Unfortunately, this is a trigger word for a lot of women who only see the word negatively. It's also here where some men misinterpret what a woman's role as an *ezer neged* means.

'The Lord God said, "It is not good for the man to be alone. I will make a helper suitable for him"' (Genesis 2:18 *NLT*). God created a woman to fill the void in Adam's life. He called her a 'helper'. '"At last!" the man exclaimed. "This one is bone from my bone, and flesh from my flesh! She will be called "woman"'' (Genesis 2:23 *NLT*).

Please permit me to invite you to think about this for a second: when God created Adam's *ezer neged*, Eve, Adam didn't see her as less than him. He didn't necessarily need someone to cook for him, clean up after him, care for him or do his chores. That wasn't the problem. Though the dynamics are different today from in the Garden of Eden, the fundamentals remain the same. The void in Adam's life was companionship. He needed a woman to complement him – to work with him, rule the earth with him, love with him, procreate with him and, after the Fall, struggle with him. I can't help but think God could have easily decided that all the beasts of the fields and all the birds of the air were enough company for Adam. They were all brought to him to be named, after all. The adjustment might have been easier for Adam, but God decided Adam needed a *woman*.

Megan continued by sharing a story with me: 'I was recently "schooled" by a friend of mine who's known me for 14 years and has pursued me for the same period. Long story short, he's very traditional and in modern-day society could be seen as primitive by the feminist mindset. Being the cheeky person I am, I have a habit of being quick to challenge when I feel schooled or reprimanded.

'He then lost interest in me for this very reason and explained, "When a woman constantly challenges or fights a man all the time, he stops seeing her as a woman but as another man. It becomes like arguing with another man. You stop having the respect you should have for her."

'This made me stop and think, "I don't want to be treated like a man". I came to realise that some aspects of my feminist nature rob me of the joy of being a lady and being treated as such. We must learn the lessons from our misfortunes, otherwise our past mishaps were pointless. I now know that I don't have to always argue with a man on every single point, even when I'm right. Sometimes there's more strength in being silent in the midst of our battle. To tame the tongue means victory for the relationship in that moment. Sometimes a man just needs to feel like he's the man, the decision maker, the leader, and that you trust him in those roles. In our "softness", God has given us the ability to redirect, sway and keep our men calm. It's about perfecting the timing of knowing when to speak and when to keep quiet. This, essentially, is where I'm weak or powerful in my identity as a woman. If he's the head and I'm the neck, we must communicate. The head can only go where the neck turns through divine communication and respect for their respective functions.

'I need to bring this tongue of mine to submission … that's often difficult, I'll confess. I'm now aware that not answering back doesn't rob me of my power, as I once thought. Choosing to become a woman of noble character[4] places me in a position to be blessed in my household,' she concluded.

I was in awe and humbled by *Megan's* honesty and her ruthless introspection. While your story may be different or you may not agree with her approach, in my opinion this is the everyday struggle for a lot of women in today's society: to balance being a submissive wife and a feminist. We all have limits within our respective genders and we must realise that this too is okay. Here we have an opportunity to complement each other as man and woman. For example, as a man, I will never give birth, and as a woman, you'll never father a child.

* * *

Here's a sad reality: there are couples I know of, and

---

4   See Proverbs 31:10–31: 'A Woman of Noble Character'.

I'm sure you do too, that 'perform' in the presence of company, showing a we're-so-in-love front, but as soon as they're alone together are at total loggerheads. That's not what love is about. If this is your situation, I'm sure that's not what you signed up for or what you envisioned your relationship to be. So why do you accept it?

I'm always touched when I see old couples holding hands, sitting in a park or restaurant, and proudly, yet silently, sharing their affection and tenderness with each other. It gives you hope that a happily-ever-after is possible, doesn't it? Well, it is. Those old couples are reaping the rewards of committed years of love and respect, with unrelenting and faithful prayers. One can immediately see how in sync and comfortable they are, such as when she places a restaurant order on his behalf, without needing to ask what he'd like to have, or when she wipes food off his beard and follows this with a quick peck and a smile that says 'I got you'. None of this behaviour is seen as offensive by the man. It's appreciated with a look that says, 'What would I do without you?', while he cuts up her food for her. The rhythm of their lives is displayed through these actions. The honesty and unconditional love with which they have travelled together manifests itself in this romantic inseparability in their later years.

Your relationship is for you, not a show for others. You may put on a façade around company but, in the long run, you're sadly simply lying to yourselves and those around you. In the interim, your lives are wasting away. That precious time can never be recouped.

Seek help where necessary and live your lives honestly. You deserve and owe it to yourselves to experience lasting, deep love. Often a man's greatness is the result of the woman in his life. Her good qualities, behaviour, strength and actions complement his and help to make him great.

In my opinion, it's your responsibility as a man to teach your lady how to treat you based on your actions towards her. This is then reciprocated, allowing her to also be herself wholly without feeling that she has to 'dumb down' for your comfort, or for you to feel like a man.

Often, the challenge for a man is to love a woman enough to make her feel enough, while some women struggle to be 'naked' and vulnerable. Sometimes it's the scars from a previous relationship or upbringing that impact both parties involved. This may cause both man and woman to be uncomfortable – a woman with her *ezer* role, and a man to value her as his *ezer*. I've come to realise that intimacy is hard for the broken, and love is difficult to understand for those who have not experienced it at its fullest: *agape* love. *Agape* love is Christ-like; it's unconditional. Jesus showed *agape* love and commands his followers to do likewise.

FOR HER

I love women and gladly join William Golding in saying, 'I think women are foolish to pretend to be equal to men, they're far superior and always have been'. I'm the kind of man who firmly believes women should never consider themselves any less than men because of their gender. What you may lack in physical strength, you more than make up for in intellect. An alpha male gladly appreciates an alpha female as he's not threatened by her and is confident in who he is. He's comfortable with her teaching him how to love her. He edifies his queen and practices mutual respect, and is equally comfortable in humbly teaching her how to love him. As men, it's important to celebrate and give recognition to your woman when you're alone together, without the company of others for show.

Ladies, it's okay to be empowered while understanding that you never have to be disrespectful or demeaning towards your man, or men in general.

A boy becomes a man
through his actions.

When does a young boy become a man?

B ecoming a man isn't just about being born male, surviving puberty or reaching a certain age milestone. A boy becomes a man through his actions. He takes full responsibility for his behaviour and carries himself in a mature way. He's not afraid of his emotions, nor is he afraid to be vulnerable and get emotional support from his woman, if that's what he needs at that moment. And he doesn't meaninglessly throw the phrase 'I love you' around when he's not ready to take on the responsibility that comes with that proclamation. The refined player shows emotion constructively. He doesn't completely shut down and is not afraid to show when he's feeling down, angry, upset or even jealous about another man being on his turf. He's equally not afraid to shed some tears, or to express unhappiness about a situation. He is the master of his emotions and expresses them truthfully. In turn, his woman can respond with genuine truth towards any subject. Women need men to be more emotionally plugged in. Women I interviewed reported that these are some of the qualities they found to be most attractive in a man:

Shelly, my florist in Los Angeles, stated, 'I find a man's strength attractive … both physical and emotional. A man who is not afraid to show his emotions or his softer side, a man who is thoroughly comfortable in his own skin, is eminently attractive.'

'Oh, yeah! Very sexy and appealing,' added *Carla*, her fellow florist. 'Women don't want to be digging or begging you for information when something is quite evidently the matter with you. If you've had a crap day or something has angered you, just say so. Share the details with us,' she concluded.

Responses such as 'I'm okay' are not only immature and irritating, they are also disheartening, especially when your woman is offering to listen or even help. Don't be afraid to show emotions with the notion that she just won't get it. Women are the masters when it comes to emotions. I know as men we've always been physical creatures. As young boys we'd just take it outside and fight it out when another guy pissed us off. The challenge is when we're with a woman and we don't know how to express ourselves emotionally without having a physical outlet. Sadly, some boys, yes, I said it, *boys*, become physically abusive towards their women. If this is you, I could never respect you or see you as a man. We must learn to express ourselves without violence, especially towards our women and children. If you do not, you remain a boy, so man up and seek help through therapy if necessary. Your abuse towards a woman may make her fearful of you but it is not her respecting you, nor is it her loving you. Men demand respect, women demand love. When you show her love, she responds with respect.

* * *

Another area that shows the difference between men and boys is in the realm of honesty. Let's keep it real. All women (and men) have major issues with being lied to. The hurt of someone lying to you ruins trust and it often never recovers. The more honest, sincere and respectful you are to the person you're with, the less you have to lie. Most women take their relationship and the responsibilities relating to it very seriously. They too get tempted. Daily they have other men coming at them; in fact, often more men than the women who come at you. They just choose to be faithful, respecting of you and respecting of themselves and your relationship. Some of my female interviewees went as far as to say they felt they are often too transparent and trustworthy and that's probably why they're taken for granted.

These women would appreciate it if men would treat them with the same level of respect, tenderness and love as they'd want another man to treat their sister, daughter or mother. They'd like to remind you that they're another man's little princess and sometimes the queen to your son or daughter. If you don't think she's worth being treated respectfully and with love, why are you with her? If you think she's not deserving of you treating her as the queen or princess she is, permit me again to ask the question, why are you with her?

Sandra, a very good friend from South Africa, said, 'Women dislike having to mother the men in their lives. A woman doesn't like constantly reminding you what you should or shouldn't be doing. If a woman has taken the time to communicate what things she has an issue with, and these are within your control, and you've done nothing about these issues (or did them just once or twice) and expect to be reminded of them, this quickly becomes frustrating for both parties.

'You get irritated at her constant "nagging" and she gets irritable from repeating herself. This translates to her that you don't care or pay enough attention to take mental notes.'

A refined player is confident in all aspects of his life, and women love that in a man. If you're not confident in your own skin, be obedient, diligent and honest enough to fix the things that need fixing. Naturally, she wants you looking your best, and that doesn't necessarily mean being the guy on the cover of *Men's Health*, though that'd be a bonus. We all want the better-looking, finer things in life, and when it comes to a relationship there should be no compromise.

In fact, a woman just wants a man who is comfortable with all aspects of his life, whether it's financially, physically or emotionally. If you are emotionally disturbed, you can't fully open up to someone else. If you're not financially stable, it will make you uncomfortable, which will detract from your confidence. We don't often admit it but our physical appearance affects our wellbeing, and if our wellbeing is affected, our confidence is threatened.

Without realising it, both men and women unconsciously transfer our lack of confidence to our partners. We may, for example, look in the mirror and not find what we see as attractive. We then ask, 'How can my partner find me attractive when I don't feel appealing?' This leads us to think from an area of insecurity, where we worry about the people we see our partners gushing over in magazines or on television, or the strangers we catch them throwing sneaky looks at in public.

I've always encouraged openness and honesty in my relationships. It's important for me that my woman knows she can talk to me about anything. Regardless of what it may be. I'm prepared for the side effects of that, too. My lived experience has taught me that in confident and comfortable relationships partners often comment on the attractiveness of people walking by. The level of comfort and confidence I speak of here is, for example, when you're sitting at a restaurant and you see a beautiful man or woman – you're both able to express your appreciation without either partner feeling jealous or inadequate. Ultimately, we need to be obedient and disciplined about getting healthy to the level and size we consider best for us. When we achieve this, we are able to live radiantly, knowing, without arrogance, that we're sexy, confident and comfortable in our own skin.

This is visible and attractive to those we come in contact with.

In the same way you want your partner or shag mate looking their best, they want the same for you.

Here's where I say: you have to be brutally honest with yourself when you meet someone. Make sure your values and views are the same on God and religion, morals, health, hygiene and finance, to name only a few. You can't just decide to let it slide and think, 'This is just a fleeting encounter'. The fact is, you never know the level of relationship that an encounter may lead to. You just never know what complications may follow from compromising early on. You have to ensure whoever you hook up with meets the level of your one-stop shop.

The issue of defining masculinity must be within the framework of how a male navigates his personal space and understands his role, responsibilities, rights and obligations.

Masculinity

Men complain daily, 'My manhood and masculinity are under threat.' Yes, they are! Because a lot of men use these terms without knowing their meaning.

What we have in today's society are a lot of physically grown boys who refuse to grow up mentally and emotionally or simply don't know how to. They weren't taught how to be grown men. This often goes back to a boy's childhood. We often find that a boy's father was absent or he himself simply didn't know how to raise a man. Sometimes it's because there were no reputable father figures or males present at all.

It's appalling when you look at the number of fathers who refuse to step up and commit to being dads or who don't take ownership of their children. As the saying goes, 'Any man can be a father, but it takes a special man to be a dad.'

Don't be seen as a sperm donor when you didn't intentionally donate your sperm at a sperm bank. Fathering is an act of nature and it's easy to do. It's often unintentional. Being a father is biological while being a dad means you're there to establish an emotional relationship.

Seek to be a dad who is there to nurture. Paying child support on time, taking care of the bills and supplying food and money doesn't make you a dad, although those things are very important. Being a dad means you play an active role in your child's development and overall growth. It means being there for your child always as best you can and ensuring he or she lacks nothing. It means being present at the pivotal moments in your child's life. It means being present at your child's games and practice sessions, teaching them how to ride a bike, how to drive a car, how to tie their shoelaces and teaching your sons how to be gentlemen and kings, who treat women as ladies and make them feel like the queens they are. It means being there to take him to church or your place of worship, to prepare him for his first date, or to give your daughter away on her wedding day. It means being there to provide guidance, a caring heart and an ever-listening ear.

Women are frustrated with men who aren't taking on their responsibilities or who keep abandoning them. Therefore, when a woman is wearing the pants and getting things done herself we shouldn't be offended. Does that mean that she wouldn't benefit from a man by her side? No! It's the lack thereof that's led her to take action on her own. Can we really blame her for trying and often succeeding at what she needs done by herself, when a vast majority of men aren't doing their job as they should, being the man in her life? Since when is it acceptable for a man to walk out on his responsibilities as the head of his household? When did we become comfortable with the terms stay-at-home dad and househusband, instead of men working so we're able to provide for our family, as a man should?

There are, of course, some dads who stay at home because they genuinely can't find a job. But we shouldn't be comfortable with this situation or use it as an excuse when we have the opportunity to work. If you're out of a job and are helping out at home because you can't afford a nanny, you should actively be searching for a job that will allow you to afford a nanny so you can both spend time with the child or children as a family. Again, I am old school when it comes to these things. I've found it more beneficial for the child or children to be with a stay-at-home mom. Since when is it okay for a man to be the primary caregiver and homemaker while his woman is the one out there working?

The number of stay-at-home dads is staggering. In June 2014, a release by the Pew Research Centre[5] found that there are 2 million stay-at-home dads in the United States. This number has doubled since their 1989 survey. It must be noted, however, that these numbers are based entirely on unemployment statistics. Nonetheless, it defined them as 'men ages 18–69 who are living with their own child or children (biological, step or adopted) younger than 18, not employed for pay in the prior year. Fathers who live apart from their children are not included.'

I know within this number are men who genuinely don't mind working, but just can't find a job. The concern is the guy who just doesn't want to work. Period. We can't be comfortable with our women doing the job we should be doing then get upset, or say, 'We're being robbed of our masculinity'. Can you blame her for acting like the man when she's taken on your role – doing what you should be doing?

* * *

I belong in the kitchen. You belong in the kitchen. There's food in the kitchen. As long as there's food in the kitchen, we both need to eat and, therefore, we both belong in the kitchen! What I'm saying is, let's share the responsibilities and take care of each other.

---

5   Available at: http://www.pewsocialtrends.org/2014/06/05/growing-num-ber-of-dads-home-with-the-kids/

I'll share a story with you. I recently visited a friend who was visibly out of shape. I asked *Alex* what had caused him to be so out of shape from the last time I'd seen him. He laughed and bashfully explained that he'd been eating a lot of takeaways and not working out. I quickly told him he needs to fix the situation for his overall wellbeing. He explained that he didn't live with his new girlfriend and when she visits, she hardly ever cooks.

She quickly defended herself, explaining, 'He's the one who doesn't want me to cook and prefers we eat takeaway. He's very fussy about what he eats and I can't make the food he enjoys from his culture.'

I laughed and asked, 'Do you love him? Do you enjoy cooking or want to cook for him?'

'Yes!' she answered.

'Then why haven't you taken the time to learn from him or his sister how to make at least one or two dishes he enjoys?'

'He can't cook.'

'Can't cook?' I interjected with disbelief. I believe all men should know how to cook. You don't have to be a chef but you should at least know the basics.

'No, he can't cook. But, you're right; I'll ask his sister for help.'

She sighed and continued, 'He's also lazy and doesn't want to help me out around the house. When I do cook, he doesn't even help with the dishes.' I can see things were getting tense.

'Why don't you help her with the dishes?' I asked.

'Never! That's not how things are done in my culture,' he explained proudly. I realised that this is one of the mistakes so many men make when it comes to the cultural norms they were exposed to growing up, versus doing what's right.

'Are you dating her or are you dating your culture?' I asked. There was silence on his part and the look on her face said she welcomed my question.

I'm not saying we should ignore or lose the core values that make us who we are as men, or our cultural upbringing for that matter. I'm saying, know when to make an executive decision to help your woman out because it's the right thing to do. It has nothing to do with culture, but rather, what's appropriate in the moment and for your relationship.

Men must have an understanding first and foremost of their role and their masculinity. You can't enter a relationship and only then hope to find yourself. You have to have discovered who you are, or be in the process of unravelling who you are, before taking on any committed relationship. When I think of masculinity and how it's sometimes defined, I'm at times troubled by the cultural context that I was exposed to growing up in Jamaica and in South Africa, where masculinity is often based on and defined by how many women you're sexually involved with.

The issue of defining masculinity must be within the framework of how a male navigates his personal space and understands his role, responsibilities, rights and obligations, as well as within the framework of the concept of himself and other men. If we don't understand ourselves, it doesn't make sense to even try and understand others. We must look at the state of our own masculinity and walk in confidence of our God-given gender, talents, abilities and blessings. In doing so, we aren't threatened by the opinions of others or their success. It's about being confident in your skin. We understand that we don't lose who we are because we know ourselves individually and collectively.

This means, if you're sharing a space, you know your role. If you're on your own, you know who you are and are comfortable with yourself when solitude is required.

Perhaps, as men, we don't take the opportunity often enough to get to know who we are inside. As part of defining and refining our masculinity, we must take the time to learn and observe behaviour across cultures. We must comprehend that part of the process of becoming or unbecoming is observing behaviour.

You must be able to ask yourself, 'What is it that my inner being is saying to me around the morality clause of what's right or what's wrong in a given situation or moment?' and be able to answer correctly. If you're unable to do this, you'll find yourself confronted with capricious sociocultural patterns and ways of life, where they thus coexist in what your lived experiences are. The lived experience for each individual is different yet the expectation is often general and it shouldn't be.

We must grasp that each person is unique, with altered requirements as the years go by. What people need from their one-stop shop is therefore different. If, for example, a woman tells a man that she's looking for someone who is always faithful, loyal and trustworthy, those are what she needs from her one-stop shop.

A lot of men may say, 'It's just not normal for a man to have only one woman. That's why I can't be faithful.' We must understand that cheating is a choice, which a lot of men make, unfortunately, hiding behind the excuse that, for men, cheating is instinctive and innate.

Well, guess what? Women have the same options available to them and, while admittedly some do cheat, the wider majority don't. They prefer not to and take pride in controlling themselves while remaining faithful to their partners.

The uncomfortable truth here is that a lot of men,

and some women, don't even try to be faithful. They may simply tell themselves that they've been burned before and therefore they don't care. Or they have the attitude that, 'What they don't know, won't hurt them.' Or they simply take on what I consider to be a selfish belief system: that it's their life and they can do what they feel, without acknowledging the potential harm they may cause in the long run if the truth should ever surface.

I strongly believe that if that is your mindset, you shouldn't be in a relationship. With being single comes the freedom to do as you please. But to live this way while you're in a relationship is self-centred, self-seeking, inconsiderate and dangerous. Shockingly enough, there are still people in today's society who don't even take the necessary precautions to protect themselves, the person they're with or their partners at home from sexually transmitted infections when they commit their infidelities.

We must understand that as we grow older, wiser and more mature, our priorities are going to change.

Does that mean that if you get married, you must change the friends you keep? Not necessarily. It just means that you're not going to do the things you used to do with them anymore. And, as the saying goes, some are for a reason, some are for a season and some for a lifetime. The way I see it, some are just for a fleeting moment. Not all blessings are meant to last the whole journey, and some are. Some blessings don't stick around if they've already served their purpose.

The same can be said for relationships. Sometimes a man or woman comes into our life for a season, sometimes for a moment, sometimes to prepare us for someone else, sometimes to show us who we truly are, sometimes to make us better men and women holistically, and sometimes, just sometimes, we're blessed to have someone come along and stay forever. We must accept the importance and take on the responsibilities our roles produce to be the ideal man or woman once we've become a refined player, a well-adjusted husband or life partner.

As I said before, when you enter into a relationship, you, as a one-stop shop, must fulfil each other's every need and craving. But men often make the mistake of thinking, 'It's all about what I want'. Wrong! Here again is why it's important that you make it clear atop of the relationship, when you compare your shelves, what things you must have in your one-stop shop and just won't live without. For example, if you consider yourself a nymphomaniac or can't live without oral sex, state that from the get-go.

As regards the connections between sex and masculinity, I'm a firm believer that a man must take pride in his performance in the bedroom: you must pay attention to your woman's body and her needs sexually. But don't fall into the masculinity ego trap; recognise as men that while it's important to know how to use your penis, it doesn't define your masculinity. You're not going into battle. There's a thin line between beating the punani up in utter pleasure and hurting your woman – pay attention and listen to her. If she tells you you're hurting her, believe you are. I know you may think that the fast-paced bang, bang, bang moves you see in your favourite porn flick are the way to go, but that isn't always the case (although sometimes it sure is). Love the punani, caress the punani, more importantly, pay attention to *her* punani and not what worked on a previous punani.

Your job is to please each other, not to have her climb the walls and run away from you because you've been hurting her to prove you have a big dick. That creates more harm and discomfort than pleasure. She wants you to pleasure her, not harm her.

I grew up hearing songs like Shabba Ranks's 'Hard and Stiff', which states that she is looking for a 'womb turner'. Seriously? What would make anyone think a woman is looking for a 'womb turner'? That's ridiculous!

Sex is meant to be a memorable experience always, not a traumatic one. Aim to get her excited at the thought of having sex with you, not bracing herself for trauma, or scared of sex in general. The understanding we need to have is that we're going into a relationship, serious or otherwise, to satisfy each other pleasurably as a team, to let each other experience levels of pleasure that should be savoured and treasured.

As a refined player and life partner, the only battle you should be fighting is for each other's wellbeing: to take care of each other and have each other's backs. The problem, often, comes back to the fact that socialisation and the male ego can cause masculinity to be misunderstood as only having to do with a man's prowess. This is why men who are prone to defining, or confining, masculinity to only having to do with their penises will encounter serious challenges. Not only do these types of men constantly feel the need to prove something but they fail to realise that their penis is auxiliary to their masculinity; it does not define it.

If you were brought up in a specific country, environment or culture that has created a negative aura around you, that doesn't mean you have to maintain it. If, for example, you grew up watching your dad beating up your mom, that doesn't mean you have to repeat that behaviour. Or if your dad or mom was an alcoholic, that doesn't mean that's who you have to become. We must choose how we live our lives. What has happened to you is your lived experience, not who you are. We all have different lived experiences and we attach different meanings to those experiences. Different meanings are attached to different things and different people. What one person's lived experiences might be, to someone else might be a humorous tale.

You are who and what you consciously choose to become. I didn't grow up with my father around all the time. I think he started out doing a great job and faltered along the way. He stopped doing his job as a dad and gave up on his responsibilities, in my opinion (he may tell you he did his best). This has lit a fire within me to better prepare for my children when I'm blessed with them and to provide them with the best life I can. I chose father figures that embodied what I felt a true dad should be and I looked up to them. As I said before, sometimes even great movie fathers were enough.

My point is that we must choose the lives we live and the type of men we are in society and the world over. We must pride ourselves in being great men. This can only be achieved through our actions in our everyday life. Respect. It isn't just given, but rather, it's earned. Stop wishing and start taking responsibility. You must be honest with yourself and stop blaming others and your circumstances. I understand that facing the truth isn't always easy, and it's sometimes scary to see all our flaws exposed. But only when we embrace our flaws and scars can they heal and lose the power they hold over us. Only then can we be comfortable and confident within our own skin, without feeling the need to be validated, or feel it necessary to fight for our place, instead of just knowing each of us carries a unique barcode and has been placed here for a specific purpose. Accept your truth, take responsibility and start living a peaceful life.

From him to her: A reminder for each day of the month	From her to him: A reminder for each day of the month
1. I need your unconditional respect (it's how I see and translate love).	1. I need your unconditional love (through that comes your respect).
2. I can be jealous when things seem out of place with you and other men.	2. I can be jealous when things seem out of place with you and other women.
3. Not all of us are cheaters. However, if I get to the point where I cheat on you once, chances are I'll do it again. I do have genuine platonic relationships with other women with no ulterior motives. Trust me to handle my business. You saying, 'I trust you. I don't trust her' really says you don't trust me or think I can't handle the temptation.	3. Not all of us are cheaters. However, if I get to the point where I cheat on you once, chances are I'll do it again. I do have genuine platonic relationships with other men with no ulterior motives. Because I have a close guy friend, doesn't mean we're fucking. When I love you, I love you and only you can change that with your actions and behaviour.

From him to her: A reminder for each day of the month	From her to him: A reminder for each day of the month
4. Men are emotional, even the really macho ones. I find it more uncomfortable to express my emotions because I'm a more physical being and I don't want to come across as 'soft'.	4. Women are emotional beings, even the ones who pretend to be tough. I take the things that matter to me to heart.
5. Acknowledge and appreciate my apology.	5. It sucks to feel like you're anticipating me doing something wrong because you think, if I've done it before I'll do it again.

From him to her: A reminder for each day of the month	From her to him: A reminder for each day of the month
6. Communication matters to me a whole lot. It's important to speak about the things you don't like about me or the relationship. I don't always pick up on subtle cues; please be direct. We won't always know what you want unless you tell us. Tell us in a clear and gentle way that doesn't bruise our egos – we'll listen and make the adjustments ... or at least try.	6. Communication matters to me a whole lot. It's important to speak about the things you don't like about me or the relationship. I don't always pick up on subtle cues. Your one-word answers are annoying. Say when you're not okay. I don't want to be digging things out of you when it's obvious you're not okay.
7. Treating you like an equal doesn't give you the right to be disrespectful or forget who the man in the relationship is.	7. Don't take my silence and submission as stupidity.

From him to her: A reminder for each day of the month	From her to him: A reminder for each day of the month
8. Please know who you are and have a vision of the kind of relationship you want to experience before you commit to a relationship. Learn to be selfless and understand that a relationship is not just for you. Things won't always go your way but they can still work.	8. Please know who you are and have a vision of the kind of relationship you want to experience before you commit to a relationship. Learn to be selfless and understand that a relationship is not just for you. Things won't always go your way but they can still work.
9. I may seem calm and secure but a compliment from you goes a long way. Think before you speak and put yourself on the receiving end of all the words you're about to say and your actions.	9. I may seem calm and secure but a compliment from you goes a long way. Think before you speak and put yourself on the receiving end of all the words you're about to say and your actions.
10. I find a woman who is aware of herself, confident, settled and in a relationship with God very appealing.	10. I find a man who is aware of himself, confident, settled and in a relationship with God simply irresistible.

From him to her: A reminder for each day of the month	From her to him: A reminder for each day of the month
11. Practice gentleness, kindness, affection, genuineness, love, respect, selflessness, trust, patience and having good priorities.	11. Practice gentleness, kindness, affection, genuineness, love, respect, selflessness, trust, patience and having good priorities.
12. I need my space. That doesn't mean I care about you or love you any less. I just need to relax and recharge for a little.	12. I need my space. When I'm out with my girls, I'm recharging.
13. Don't try to manipulate me with sex when you've messed up. Just acknowledge when you're wrong.	13. Don't only buy me gifts on special occasions or flowers only when you've done something wrong.

From him to her: A reminder for each day of the month	From her to him: A reminder for each day of the month
14. If I've messed up and you say you forgive me, do so purely or don't do it at all. I'm not saying it's easy, but you must respect and honour your decision. You can't keep using it against me. You may not say it, but your actions and attitude do. When I've forgiven you, don't live with guilt anticipating I'll do something wrong so you can feel even. Don't think I'm too good to be true. We should be too good to be true to each other.	14. If I've messed up and you say you forgive me, do so purely or don't do it at all. I'm not saying it's easy, but you must respect and honour your decision. You can't keep using it against me. You may not say it, but your actions and attitude do. When I've forgiven you, don't live with guilt anticipating I'll do something wrong so you can feel even. Don't think I'm too good to be true. We should be too good to be true to each other.
15. I want you to be my personal pornstar.	15. I aim to be the personal pornstar you seek deep down.

From him to her: A reminder for each day of the month	From her to him: A reminder for each day of the month
16. Be confident in your skin and take charge. Play rough when necessary and please talk dirty to me. It's okay to talk dirty to me and roleplay once in a while!	16. Be confident in your skin and take charge. Play rough when necessary, please talk dirty to me and try new things. It's okay to talk dirty to me and roleplay once in a while!
17. I need you to be my CEO: Chief Encouragement Officer.	17. It's totally okay to break down and cry in front of me if necessary (just not all the time – and yes, some of us do take advantage and see it as weakness).
18. Contrary to popular belief, I take commitment seriously once I've made the decision to commit.	18. Contrary to popular belief, I'm not always after a commitment and may occasionally only be looking for a good time.

From him to her: A reminder for each day of the month	From her to him: A reminder for each day of the month
19. I want a woman who supports my dreams and encourages me to succeed. Don't always focus your energy on my weaknesses; compliment my strengths and show appreciation.	19. I want a man who supports my dreams and encourages me to succeed. Don't always focus your energy on my weaknesses; compliment my strengths and show appreciation.
20. Great relationships don't just happen; they are built by two willing, committed, hardworking, loyal and faithful individuals, who are willing to compromise.	20. Great relationships don't just happen; they are built by two willing, committed, hardworking, loyal and faithful individuals, who are willing to compromise.
21. If we have a disagreement, make-up sex is appreciated.	21. If we have a disagreement, make-up sex is appreciated.
22. I think about sex ... a lot. I fantasise about sex far more than you do. And yes, more casually than you do. This doesn't mean I'm sleeping with all the women I can.	22. I may not think about sex as much as you do. But I do fantasise and I, sure as hell, love sex as much as you do ... if it not more.

From him to her: A reminder for each day of the month	From her to him: A reminder for each day of the month
23. Treat me like a king and I'll inevitably treat you like a queen.	23. Treat me like a queen and I'll inevitably treat you like a king.
24. I love foreplay, unless it's a quickie of course. When going down on me please do it with passion. I know when you're not enjoying it.	24. I love foreplay, unless it's a quickie of course. When going down on me please do it with passion. I know when you're not enjoying it.
25. Mow the lawn and practice being well-groomed. I need you looking royal at all times.	25. Prune the hedges and practice being well-groomed. I need you looking royal at all times.
26. Don't leave me hanging once you've come, with a 'sort yourself out' attitude, while you lie there like a plank.	26. If it happens that you come first, find other ways to ensure I come too. You don't want a grumpy woman around you, trust me.

From him to her: A reminder for each day of the month	From her to him: A reminder for each day of the month
27. Please initiate sex! Don't confuse my dick with *Ian's*, *John's* or *Zakes's* dick. Get to know me and my dick. What I love, what turns me on and what I enjoy. Because the men from your past liked or loved something doesn't mean I will. Read my body language and don't be offended if I tell you how to do what I like when we're having sex.	27. My punani is not *Samantha's*, *Chloe's* or *Puleng's* punani. Get to know me and my punani – what gets me wet, what I love and what I enjoy. Because the women from your past liked or loved something doesn't mean I will. Ask if you're not sure how to do certain things. Read my body language and don't be offended if I tell you how to do what I like when we're having sex.
28. I prefer an open-minded woman who enjoys to put it down and is exploratory. When we're using sex toys, be aware that they are there to spice things up. Don't make me feel inadequate.	28. I prefer an open-minded man who enjoys to put it down and is exploratory. Don't be frightened of sex toys, they're not there to replace you, they're there to spice things up.

From him to her: A reminder for each day of the month	From her to him: A reminder for each day of the month
29. I don't want to cuddle immediately after sex. Give me a few minutes to come down from my high.	29. I want us to cuddle after sex or be tended to for a little while.
30. I want you to live by the same code as me: to be, rather than to seem. Be yourself always – stop trying so hard to be what you think I'm looking for. Façades don't last forever. Once I've fallen for your façade, that's who I know as 'you'.	30. I want you to live by the same code as me: to be, rather than to seem. Be yourself always – stop trying so hard to be what you think I'm looking for. Façades don't last forever. Once I've fallen for your façade, that's who I know as 'you'.
31. I want to be your one-stop shop!	31. I want to be your one-stop shop!

Finding the men and women we look to find begins with us. Live your life in a manner that mirrors the partner you seek to find.

Last word

This book was written through my lived experiences and observations along with the opinions shared with me through conversations with friends and interviews with random men and women in the interest and hope of finding the answers and solutions to our selfish behaviour that often hurts the ones who love us, the ones who simply need their unconditional loyalty, love and respect to be reciprocated. It is also for the women and men who want to explore with their partner but just don't know how to, or are terrified to do so out of fear of being pigeonholed as weird.

In writing this book, I wanted to spark conversations among ourselves about the uncomfortable truths we face in our relationships but may be too scared to mention to the partners with whom we share, or hope to share, our happily-ever-after. It is for us to realise that our partners should be our best friend and our one-stop shop: that one person we can speak to about everything. The person we can explore with, devoid of feeling judged or inadequate.

We must realise that no one person can fulfil all our emotional needs. Have you ever stopped to notice how different each of your friends is? That's because they all have and offer something different: humour, perspective, honesty and personality. Allow them to fulfil their purpose. To expect one person to fulfil us is simply unfair, unreasonable and unrealistic. Your parents play a specific role. So does each friend individually; in the same manner, our partners are there to complement us.

In the interest of keeping this book's 'real talk' theme there are specific things I chose not to speak on in detail, for example, fatherhood and marriage, as I haven't lived those experiences yet.

This book will not give you all the answers you seek. It will, however, make you a better man or woman. It will get you closer to the happiness you long for. It promises a life that's more rewarding, caring, loving and nurturing to ourselves and our partners.

Change is necessary when striving to become better. Finding the men and women we look to find begins with us. Live your life in a manner that mirrors the partner you seek to find. I think women are good listeners. But so are men. Society, however, is constructed in a manner where men tell women what they want to hear, rather than what they need to hear. The truth! A caged bird still knows how to fly. It is its position that isn't conducive to taking flight. But nature always takes its course. Women are wired to respond. If you treat her with love she will reciprocate it tenfold. But, if you ridicule her and her love, what you get back will be 10 times worse.

Sifiso, a South African friend of mine, once said to me, 'Women are like incubators, *mfethu* (brother). They provide a nurturing environment of care and protection only as long as they're efficiently maintained. Give her food ingredients and she'll give you a meal, give her a house and she'll give you a home, infuse her with healthy sperm and she'll bear you children. Give her hell, however, and she'll show you the devil.'

Love her. Respect him. You'll always hear a woman say, 'He doesn't love me enough', while a man will always say, 'She doesn't respect me enough'. Women see love as just that: love. She demands it. Men, on the other hand, as I have observed, translate love as respect and demand it. I do ... and I will never compromise on it. It is through *agape* love and prayer that we become the best men and women for our partners. We're able to nurture them, care for them, love them unconditionally and respect them purely. It's here that we lead each other boldly. It's here that we serve each other humbly. It's here that we cherish each other deeply. It's here that we function as each other's one-stop shop.

I look forward to sharing my new lived experiences with you as I embark on the next dimension of my life. I have now taken on the responsibility to be the incredible man I was created to be.

Until then, love, peace and blessings.

Stevel Marc

.

Stevel Marc is a Jamaican-born, international model and actor, who spends his time between South Africa and Los Angeles.

"I strongly believe this book is bigger than me. You're holding this book for a reason. There are no coincidences; you're holding this book because you're in the right place at the right time. It will give you the answers to the many questions you've been asking. It will bring you closer to the happiness you long for and it promises to make you a better man or woman. It will give you and your partner a more rewarding, caring, loving and nurturing life."